THE MAGICAL

Do unto othe

GIFT OF

you would have

KINDNESS

them do unto you

JOY HANEY

The Magical Gift of Kindness by Joy Haney
@ April, 1997 First Printing
April 1999, Second Printing
Radiant Life Publications

Cover design by Paul Povolni

All scripture quotations are from the King James Version of the Bible

ISBN 1-880969-28-9

Printed in the United States of America

Table of Contents

Dedication 5

1. Kindness Warms the Soul—A Collage of Stories 9
   - Story Number 1: Our Kindest City
   - Story Number 2: Teddy Bear
   - Story Number 3: Two Brothers
   - Story Number 4: Two Barber Shops
   - Story Number 5: Unarticulated Language of Love
   - Story Number 6: Half a Blanket
   - Story Number 7: He Shined His Shoes
   - Story Number 8: A New Suit

2. Kindness at Random 27
3. Kindness is Love 33
4. Kindness is Being Gentle 53
5. Kindness is Being Respectful and Courteous 71
6. Kindness is Showing Honor 91
7. Kindness is Honoring One Another 97
8. Kindness is Rewarded 119

9. Kindness—Can It Be Brought Back? 135
10. Kindness vs. Evil 151
Epilogue 159
Notes 163

Dedication

This book is dedicated to the thousands of people who have been kind to me. I would have to start with the people who first surrounded me as a child. My parents, Travis Roy and Margaret McDonald, were the kindest people I have ever met. My brother and sisters have always been close to me and very kind and thoughtful. My grandparents, Merle and Crystal Savage and John and Lillian McDonald, and my aunts, uncles and cousins have all enriched my life with kindness.

My pastor and his wife, Rev. and Mrs. J.E. Rode, were pure gold. The things they did for me will ever live in my memory. As my world widened, the teachers in grade school especially stand out to me as being kind and caring. Then the friends I grew up with and met in church, school, college and at work, even now leave me with little smiles as I remember their kindness and generosity.

When I met my husband, Kenneth Haney, he seemed to be the kindest man anywhere, aside from my father. Of course, his father and mother, Clyde and Olive Haney, and his sisters and their husbands have always been kind to me.

Our children, Sherrie, Nathaniel, Stephanie, Elizabeth and Angela truly love me and are kind to me. They and their spouses are very dear to me.

I became a pastor's wife 35 years ago, and the people that have come into my life through this ministry have shown themselves very kind and caring. The cards and sincere words of appreciation have lightened many loads. The unexpected gifts and thoughtful gestures from these dear people continue to add sunshine to my heart. I cannot begin to mention names, for there are too many to list here, but they are listed in God's records and mine.

When God opened the door for me to begin traveling and speaking several years ago, He also blessed me with many dear friends who have been precious and kind. The leaders and the unknowns, the elderly and the young, many of them have wrapped me in love and shared their heart full of love. The cards, the gifts, the letters, plaques, bookmarks, etc., are stored or displayed, and bring a glow when I remember the person, time and place.

God has given our family many dear friends within our church organization (and without), within our city, across our nation and around the world. This book is dedicated to anyone and everyone that has ever been kind to me, for you have made my life richer and lifted my load many times when you did not even know it. May God bless you richly also!

One:

Kindness Warms the Soul—A Collage of Stories

Story Number 1: "Our Kindest City"

John S. Tompkins

I had just left the fine old city hall in Rochester, N.Y., when a young woman stepped up to ask if I could change a $10 bill for her bus fare. In New York City, where I live, a young woman would be afraid to ask for change from a strange man, and a man would be suspicious if she did. But in Rochester, such happenings are part of everyday life. I smiled and made change for her.

This city of 231,000, located on Lake Ontario and home to some of America's best-known corporations, is a throwback to a kinder, gentler America. It is the sort of place where, as happened recently, a post-office employee will come out to help an absent-minded citizen retrieve a bank deposit envelope accidentally dropped in a mailbox; where a group of workmen reportedly replaced—for free—the fire-damaged roof of a neighbor who had spent years turning a wreck into a livable house; where a truck driver retrieved a child's doll from the street after it had fallen from a car, and returned it to the doll's heartbroken 2½-year-old owner.

In two unusual studies, done half a century apart, Rochester was designated the kindest city in America. The most recent survey was conducted between 1990 and 1992 by Robert V. Levine, chairman of the Psychology Department at California State University, Fresno. Levine and a group of his students studied 36 U.S. cities to find where the most helpful people live. As part of the research, the students pretended to accidentally drop something on the street, to need change, or to be blind or lame and in need of assistance. More people went out their way to be helpful in Rochester than in any other city. East Lansing, Michigan, and Nashville, Tennessee, were second and third. At the very bottom of the list was New York City.

What made the study all the more fascinating was that it echoed data from 1940. A survey examining the character of 43 American cities ranked Rochester number one in altruism.

I was irresistibly drawn there to see for myself. Ultimately I traced the city's strain of generosity back to its earliest days and to one strong, determined man.

Rochester was founded by Nathaniel Rochester, near the falls of the Genesee River. The first residents arrived in 1812, and little more than a decade later found themselves in the middle of a boom. The opening of the Erie Canal in 1825 brought a flood of people, and Rochester, now a gateway to the West, became a boisterous place of taverns and transients.

On Friday, November 13, 1829, an acrobat and daredevil named Sam Patch unwittingly began a chain of events that led to Rochester's moral rebirth. Patch was on his way home after making a spectacular and widely publicized jump from a rope ladder suspended over Niagara Falls. At Rochester, he vowed to make a 120-foot leap over the falls of the Genesee River and into the swirling waters below.

On the day of the jump, he attracted an audience of thousands. But this time, Patch apparently lost his balance. Arms whirling madly, he struck the water with a great splash. Minutes passed, but he did not surface. (His body was found in the ice the following spring.) Sobered by the tragedy, the chastened crowd quietly left the scene.

Two days after Patch's fatal jump, Josiah Bissell, one of Rochester's leading businessmen, rose solemnly to his feet in the Third Presbyterian Church and sternly warned that all "who by their presence encouraged that soul to leap into eternity will be held accountable on the Judgment Day." In the silence that followed, some in the congregation wept. Others wrote that shivers ran up and down their spines.

Sure that he had touched a nerve, Bissell determined to save Rochester's soul. He arranged to bring the Rev. Charles G. Finney, considered to be one of the greatest evangelists of the day, to Rochester for a protracted revival.

A tall, handsome figure with hypnotic eyes and a commanding voice, Finney could stare down unbelievers and silence angry mobs. The evangelist's appearance attracted almost everyone in Rochester who could walk to church. He preached or held prayer meetings almost every day. Much of the business activity in Rochester stopped. The streets emptied. Taverns closed because they had so few customers.

Finney spent six months in Rochester and converted hundreds of residents—lawyers, doctors, judges, tradesmen, bankers, boatmen, workers, master craftsmen—to born-again Christianity. He scorched their consciences and urged them not to follow the selfish way of the world. Finney angrily denounced the evils of selfishness and deliberately aimed his message at the wealthy and powerful. He got Rochester's society ladies to act as his agents by sending them all over town and persuading people to come and hear him.

Having converted the affluent, Finney's final step was to get them to direct their energy and wealth into beneficial philanthropies. He was amazingly successful. Rochester embarked on a church-building boom. Rochesterians went on to establish a university, organize charities and self-help agencies, build a public-school system, fight against slavery (the city was a station on the Underground Railroad, which smuggled slaves into Canada), form unions and reform the prison system. Rochester became a city where love for one's fellow man was more than an empty phrase.

"Charles Grandison Finney's coming to town was the pivotal experience that changed Rochester," says the Rev. Kenneth S. Fox, pastor of the Open Door Mission. Fox believes that the influence of Finney's powerful message is still felt in Rochester because it was passed down in so many different ways. Parents who heard the evangelist told their children. Ministers and Sunday School teachers carried the word to their flocks. And generation after generation of Rochesterians stayed in the city and preserved the Finney legacy.

George Eastman, the founder of Eastman Kodak, was only two when the evangelist made his last visit to Rochester in 1856. But when Eastman grew up and started his photography business, Rochester society included many important leaders who had been influenced by Charles Grandison Finney's theology of social reform. Eastman firmly believed that part of the responsibility of having money was doing good works, and that success in business and community involvement go hand in hand. He set an example that other Rochester corporations followed. By World War I, Eastman's participation in city affairs and his financial support of educational, cultural and social-service programs was so large that Rochester was called "George Eastman's town." He went on to lead the Community Chest—now called the United Way of Greater Rochester—in 1919.

As decades passed, memories of Charles Finney dimmed, but his teaching has endured and with it, Rochester's tradition of helping others. Residents give more money to United Way on a per-capita basis than residents of any other United Way region of its size. This record has stood for at least 20 years. There are more than 250 non-profit volunteer organizations, filling every conceivable need—13 supply services to the blind, 36 provide food for the needy. More Monroe County lawyers volunteer pro-bono work than those in any other county in New York State. "Rochester is full of people who are willing to help one another," says Fox, "and they're willing to bloom where they're planted."

The city lives by the golden rule in ways large as well as small. The community has its own health care system, created through cooperation among employers, doctors and hospitals, that far exceeds the national average in the percentage of residents covered, and at less cost per employee than the national average. At a time when many public schools around the country have embraced a "value free" education, the Rochester City School District adopted a policy which dictates that "kindness and caring, obligation to the public good, respect for others" and 19 other values are included in the curriculum. The school system is required to keep religion out of the classrooms, but it has also kept out free condoms. Says Harry Reis, professor of psychology at the University of Rochester: "People here don't laugh when you speak of family values."

As I got ready to leave Rochester, I heard that Eastman Kodak's chief executive had decided not to relocate headquarters of a key division to the Washington, D.C., area. Perhaps the decision is not surprising. Who would want to move away from the kindest city in the United States? [1]

Story Number 2: "Teddy Bear"

Dale Royal, Tommy Hill, Red Sovine and J. William Denny

I was on the outskirts of a little Southern town,
trying to reach my destination before the sun went down.
The old CB was blaring away on channel 1-9
when there came a little boy's voice on the radio line.
And he said, "Breaker 1-9, is anyone there?
Come on back, truckers, and talk to Teddy Bear."

Well, I keyed the mike and I said, "You got it, Teddy Bear."
And the little boy's voice came back on the air.
"'Preciate the break. Who we got on that end?"
I told him my handle and then he began.

"Now I'm not supposed to bother you fellas out there.
Mom says you're busy and for me to stay off the air.
But you see, I get lonely and it helps to talk
'cause that's about all I can do. I'm crippled I can't walk."
I came back and told him to fire up that mike
and I'd talk to him as long as he'd like.

"This was my dad's radio," the little boy said.

"But I guess it's mine and mom's now 'cause my daddy's
dead.
Dad had a wreck about a month ago.
He was trying to get home in a blinding snow.
Mom has to work now to make ends meet.
And I'm not much help with my two crippled feet.
She says not to worry, that we'll make it all right.
But I hear her crying sometimes late at night.

Ya know, there's one thing I want more than anything else to
see.
Ah, I know you guys are too busy to bother with me.
But, ya see, my dad used to take me for rides when he was
home.
But I guess that's all over now since my daddy's gone."
Not one breaker came on the ol' CB
as that little crippled boy talked with me.
I tried hard to swallow a lump; it just wouldn't stay down
as I thought about my boy back in Greenville Town.

"Dad was going to take Mom and me with him later on this
year.
Why, I remember him saying, 'Someday this ol' truck will be
yours, Teddy Bear.'

But I know I will never get to ride an 18-wheeler again.
But this old base will keep me in touch with all my trucker friends.
Teddy Bear's going to back on out now and leave you alone
'cause it's about time for Mom to come home.
But you give me a shout when you're passing through
and I'll sure be happy to come back to you."

Well, I came back and I said, "Before you go 10-10,
what's your home 20, little CB friend?"
Well, he gave me his address and I didn't once hesitate
'cause this hot load of freight is just gonna have to wait.
I turned that truck around on a dime
and headed straight for Jackson Street 229.

As I rounded the corner, I got…a shock:
Eighteen-wheelers lined up for three city blocks.
Why, I guess every driver from miles around had caught Teddy Bear's call,
and that little crippled boy was having a ball.
For as fast as one driver would carry him in,
another would carry him to his truck and take off again.
Well, you better believe I took my turn at riding Teddy Bear.
And then I carried him back in and put him down in his chair.

And Buddy, if I never live to see happiness again,
I want you to know I saw it that day in the face of that little
man.

We took up a collection for him before his momma got home.
And each driver said good-bye and then they were all gone.
He shook my hand with a mile-long grin
and said, "So long, trucker; I'll catch ya again."

I hit that interstate with tears in my eyes.
I turned on the radio and got another surprise.
"Breaker 1-9," came a voice on the air,
"just one word of thanks from Momma Teddy Bear.
We wish each and every one a special prayer for you,
'cause you just made my little boy's dream come true.
I'll sign off now before I start to cry.
May God ride with you; 10-4 and good-bye." [2]

Story Number 3: "Two Brothers"

Told by Rev. Clifford Gustafson

In 1984, Sarajevo, Yugoslavia, was the host country of the Winter Olympics. The weather was terrible—snow and sleet, melting and freezing alternately.

Phil Mahre and his younger brother, Steve, were both competing in the downhill slalom race. The skiers had to negotiate steep grades and sharp curves, all the while dodging around flags on poles driven into the snow. A large number of skiers awaited their turn atop the steep hill.

Finally it was Phil's turn. He was the better skier. But the slopes were rough, having been melted and re-frozen many times. He made it and his time was excellent. Upon reaching the bottom, he asked for a phone from one of the officials and asked to speak to his younger brother atop the hill awaiting his turn.

"Watch for turn #7. Keep to the west," he told Steve. "It's turning to slush and could cause you trouble. Beware of curve #16. It's drifting deep and I almost fell. Be careful."

Another skier spoke to Phil. "Are you out of your mind? This is the Olympics. If you help another you are lowering your own chances of winning. He now can beat your time."

Phil replied to the fellow skier, "I could not have my brother come down that treacherous slope without giving him all the help I could."

In the end Steve did well, but not as well as his older brother Phil, who won the gold medal.

Story Number 4: "Two Barber Shops"

Walter B. Knight

There were once two barber shops in a small town. One was operated by an Italian, one by a Russian. One week there was a large increase in Tony Sachetti's business. He learned that his competitor was ill. Tony worked late Saturday night. On Sunday morning he put on his best suit. He took all the money he had made above his regular intake during the week, and took it to his competitor's house. When he walked into the bedroom where the sick man was, Tony grinned real big and said, "A little cash for you, Ivan," as he poured out the bills and coins on the bed. "Get well quick!" With a laugh and warm handclasp, Tony was gone. [3]

Story Number 5: "Unarticulated Language of Love"

Walter B. Knight

One day I was visiting the gnarled, lame, and blind people who lived in the Chicago Home for the Incurables. How friendless and forgotten some of them were! I came to the bed of an aged German Jew whose face was scarred and mottled as a result of having been beaten within an inch of his life by Hitler's Gestapo. An attendant told me that he couldn't understand a word of English. I beamed compassion and kindness upon him. His face wreathed in smiles and reflected good will back to me. Linguistic barriers seemed to vanish. The unarticulated language of love and kindness fused together the hearts of two men who were from two different backgrounds. [4]

Story Number 6: "Half a Blanket"

Walter B. Knight

General Marquis de Lafayette, a Frenchman, helped General Washington when the thirteen American colonies were fighting for their freedom. After the war Lafayette returned to

France. In 1824 he visited America. An old soldier went up to him and said, "Do you remember me?"

"No," Lafayette said.

"Do you remember the frosts and snows of Valley Forge?" asked the soldier.

"I shall never forget them," answered Lafayette.

"One bitterly cold night," continued the soldier, "when you were going the rounds, you came upon a sentry who was thinly clothed. He was slowly freezing to death. You took his gun and said, 'Go to my hut. There you will find clothes, a blanket and a fire. After warming yourself, bring the blanket to me. Meanwhile I will keep guard for you.'

"When the soldier returned to you, you cut the blanket in two pieces. One piece you kept. You gave the other part to the sentry." Tears ran down the cheeks of the old soldier as he said, "General, here is that half of the blanket. I am the sentry whose life you saved." [5]

Story Number 7: "He Shined My Shoes"

Walter B. Knight

A prisoner once asked a minister who was passing his prison cell, "Do you remember me?" Before the minister could reply, the prisoner continued, "I remember you. You got me out of one of the 'dives' of New York City. You gave me a letter to a mission where I could find shelter. Before we parted, you got some clothes for me. I was shivering with delirium tremens, and couldn't dress myself. So you dressed me, and there was one thing more. After you dressed me, you said, 'You want to look nice from head to toe, so I'll shine your shoes.'

"I don't remember much what you said about Christ, because I did not want to be better. I did not want to go to the mission, and I did not want your religion, but to think that you cared enough for my soul to black my shoes—that has followed me ever since. I believe God has caused our paths to cross again. I have come to the end of myself, and I am now ready to give my life to the One whose love caused you, an honored minister, to perform that humble service when I first met you." [6]

Story Number 8: "A New Suit"

Author Unknown

A primary and intermediate school was so located as to be separated by a fence from the rear of the White House grounds. The President often watched the children play. One morning the teacher gave them a lesson in neatness, and asked each boy to come to school the next day with his shoes blacked.

They all obeyed. One of them, John S., a poor one-armed lad, had used stove polish, the only kind his home afforded. The boys were merciless in their ridicule. The boy was only nine years old, the son of a dead soldier, his mother a washerwoman, with three other children to provide for. The President heard the boys jeering Johnny and learned the facts about the boy.

The next day John came to school with a new suit and with new shoes, and told everyone that the President had called at his home and took him to the store and bought two suits of clothes for him and clothes for his sisters, and sent coal and groceries to the house. In addition to this the lad brought to the teacher a scrap of paper containing a verse of Scripture, which Mr. Lincoln had requested to have written upon the blackboard.

"Inasmuch as ye have done it unto one of the least of these my brethren, ye have done it unto me."

Some weeks after, the President visited the school, and the teacher directed his attention to the verse which was still there. Mr. Lincoln read it, then, taking a crayon said: "Boys, I have another quotation from the Bible, and I hope you will learn it and come to know its truth as I have known and felt it." Then below the other verse he wrote:

> "It is more blessed to give than to receive."
>
> A. Lincoln [7]

Two:

Kindness at Random

Adair Lara wrote an article entitled, "Practice Random Kindness and Senseless Acts of Beauty." She related how one winter day in San Francisco, a woman in a red Honda, with Christmas presents piled high in the back, drove up to the Bay Bridge toll booth and paid for herself and six cars behind her. One after another, the next six drivers arrived at the toll booth, dollars in hand, only to be told, "Some lady up ahead already paid your fare. Have a nice day."

The lady in the red Honda had read something on an index card taped to a friend's refrigerator: "Practice random kindness and senseless acts of beauty." The phrase seemed to leap out at her.

Judy Foreman spotted the same phrase a hundred miles from her home, spray-painted on a warehouse wall. She shared it with her husband, Frank, who liked it so much that he put it up on the classroom wall for his seventh graders, one of whom was the daughter of a local columnist. The columnist put it in the paper. Two days later, she heard from Anne Herbert, who had jotted the phrase down on a paper placemat in a restaurant, after turning it around in her mind for days.

A man sitting nearby said, "That's wonderful," and copied it down on his own placemat.

Now the phrase is spreading, on bumper stickers, on walls, at the bottom of letters and business cards. And as it spreads, so does much goodness. In Portland, Oregon, a man plunked a coin into a stranger's parking meter just in time. In Patterson, New Jersey, a dozen people with pails and mops and tulip bulbs descended on a run-down house and cleaned it from top to bottom while the frail elderly owners looked on, dazed and smiling. A man in St. Louis, whose car had been rear-ended by a young woman, waves her away, saying, "It's a scratch. Don't worry."

A man planted daffodils along the roadway. In Seattle, a man appointed himself a one-man vigilante sanitation service and roams the concrete hills collecting litter in a supermarket cart. In Atlanta, a man scrubbed graffiti from a green park bench.

Herbert said, "Anything you think there should be more of, do it randomly. Kindness can build on itself as much as violence can."

Adair Lara says, "You can't commit a random kindness without feeling as if your own troubles have been lightened if only because the world has become a slightly better place.…Like all revolutions, guerrilla goodness begins slowly, with a single act. Let it be yours." [1]

John Wesley wrote the following poem:

Do all the good you can
By all the means you can
In all the ways you can
In all the places you can
At all the times you can
To all the people you can
As long as ever you can! [2]

One bitter, cold day in London, an old blind man sat on a little stool near the corner of a street. His fingers were blue with cold, and he was trying to play a cheap violin. Few people paid any attention to him, or put any money in his tin cup.

Then two well-dressed men stopped. One said in broken English, "No luck, yet? Nobody give money? Make them. Play till they open!" Then he said, "Give me your violin!" The old man gave it to him and he began to play. Beautiful, heavenly music flowed from it, while men, women, boys and girls listened spell-bound. When the music stopped, a hat was passed and it was filled with money for the blind man.

When the stranger returned the violin and bow, the blind man said, "Oh, Sir, you have my undying thanks! What is your name?"

As the stranger walked away, he said, "My name is Paganini." The famous violinist had practiced spreading a random act of kindness, which lighted up many lives.

The greatest glow inside a person comes not from expecting to be repaid for a kindness, but from giving without a thought of remuneration. *Kindness always pays, but it pays most when you do not do it for pay.* William P. Barker shares an incident that illustrates that statement.

> A youthful giant slouched into an Illinois schoolroom one day after school. The teacher, Mentor Graham, looked up and recognized the young husky standing there awkwardly as the new young buck who had recently moved to town and who had whipped the daylights out of all local toughs.

Graham looked up and down the six-foot-four-inches of muscle and ignorance before him and offered to help him read and to lend him a few books. No one remembers Mentor Graham nowadays. He was one of the quiet men, but his pupil will be remembered for a long time. His name was Abraham Lincoln. [3]

Not many things can be compared to the glow that warms the heart when one does something kind for someone else. In October 1996, my husband and I experienced this glow when we were flying home together from a conference. Since we do a lot of flying we are able to accumulate many miles in frequent flyer accounts with different airlines. One of them is United Airlines, which we happened to be flying on, and with whom we are Premier members.

United had run a special promotion back in the summer and we had purchased our tickets for $109.00 round trip. Since we were Premier members, we could upgrade to first class for a small fee, which we did.

We discovered that on the same airplane were an elderly couple who were friends of ours. So I asked the flight attendant if we could trade places with them—they would come up to first class and sit in our seats, and we would go back to coach and sit in their seats. Then I went back and told them what we were trying to do, thinking that it would be fine.

The attendant came back and told us that we could not do this. Feeling disappointed, I prayed, “Lord, I place this in your hands. If You want it to be, You make a way.”

Shortly thereafter the ticket agent from inside the terminal came on the plane and asked us what we wanted to do. We told her and she looked around and saw two empty seats in first class. She had the flight attendant go back and bring our friends up to first class, and told us to stay there also. What a pleasant surprise!

When the elderly woman came up to the front, she said, “This will be my first time to ride in first class.” They were smiling and we were smiling, and there was a little glow around my heart the whole way home.

Un-premeditated kindnesses should punctuate our lives on a daily basis. Go ahead and act upon those kind impulses. They are the best investments you can make, for as the Chinese proverb says, *the fragrance lingers on the hand that gives the perfume.*

Three:

Kindness is Love

Once a rich, miserly man who was unloved in his community went to a wise man to ask why. The wise man told him to look out the window and tell him what he saw. "People," replied the rich man.

Then the wise man led him to a mirror and asked, "What do you see now?"

"Myself," answered the rich man.

Said the wise man, "In the window there is glass and in the mirror there is glass. But the glass in the mirror is covered with a film of silver. As soon as a little silver is added, you cease to see others and see only yourself."

It is people that are important: their feelings, needs and heart yearnings. When the importance of other people diminishes, then misery sets in.

A budding high-school orator delivered Lincoln's Gettysburg Address. Calmly he began, "Fourscore and seven years ago...." He glowed with fervency when he came to the climactic words "...that government *of* the people, *by* the people, and *for* the people shall not perish from the earth!" The audience applauded uproariously! An old man hobbled slowly through the crowd and said to the young orator, "You did a grand job, son! You will be interested to know that I was present at Gettysburg when Lincoln delivered that memorable speech. What an occasion it was. But, son, you didn't say it just like Lincoln did. You said, 'Government *of* the people, *by* the people, and *for* the people.' When Lincoln spoke these words—it seems I can hear him still—he said, 'Government of the *people*, by the *people*, and for the *people* shall not perish from the earth!' His emphasis and concern were on *people*. Your emphasis is on prepositions."

Walter B. Knight wrote the following:

> It was the need of *people*—not the slavish, legalistic observance of the Sabbath—which was of paramount concern to the Saviour. The sight of hungry, shepherdless

people moved the heart and hand of the Saviour in their behalf.

The spiritual and temporal needs of *people* are of greater concern to God than any institution, no matter how hoary and venerable an institution may be. This fact was enunciated with authority and finality in Christ's words: "The sabbath was made for man, and not man for the sabbath" (Mark 2:27). In countries where this principle is reversed, *people* become pawns of the state and are degraded to the level of pack animals!

When religious institutions lose their primary concern for the spiritual and temporal needs of *people*, heaven weeps and the zest to carry on fades and dies. Such institutions become soulless and are a distorted image or caricature of what they ought to be. Our major emphasis must ever be on *people*. We must love, respect, and have an unfeigned concern for people, wanting their highest and best welfare everywhere. [1]

I Corinthians 13:4 says that love is kind. Kindness can be understood by all. It is showing concern for people, caring about their plights and problems, and helping in a time of need, sadness or distress.

Often many people learn the Ten Commandments, but seem to forget the *new* commandment the Lord instituted. Many years ago a woman did just that. A minister, wanting to test the hospitality of the members of one of the churches over which he had the oversight, dressed as a tramp and went to some of their houses. Some rudely rebuffed him, saying, "Be gone!" Others showed kindness. One housewife began to lecture him, asking, "How many commandments are there?" Hesitantly, the tramp mumbled, "Eleven." The woman sent him away telling him that the next time anyone asked him how many commandments there were, to answer, "Ten."

The following Sunday when he went to the pulpit he read his text: "A new commandment I give unto you, That ye love one another; as I have loved you, that ye also love one another" (John 13:34). Then the minister said, "Friends, it would appear that with this *new commandment*, there are *eleven* commandments." The woman who had berated the minister, and sent him away telling him there were only ten commandments, was seen that Sunday with her head bowed, looking very embarrassed.

Jesus said, "By this shall all men know that ye are my disciples, if ye have love one to another" (John 13:35). Jesus also said, "...I never knew you: depart from me" (Matthew 7:23).

Could He have been saying, "Your lack of love for one another did not identify you with me"?

John said,

> He that loveth not knoweth not God; for God is love. If a man say, I love God, and hateth his brother, he is a liar; for he that loveth not his brother whom he hath seen, how can he love God whom he hath not seen? And this commandment have we from him, That he who loveth God love his brother also (I John 4:8,20-21).

Church members would be a lot better off if they adopted the words of Benjamin Franklin as their guide to conversation. He said, "I will speak ill of no man, not even in the matter of truth, but rather excuse the faults I hear charged upon others and upon proper occasions speak all the good I know of everybody."

Jesus, of course, said it best. His words shocked the religious leaders of that day.

> Judge not, that ye be not judged. For with what judgment ye judge, ye shall be judged: and with what measure ye mete, it shall be measured to you again. And why beholdest thou the mote that is in thy brother's eye, but consider-

> est not the beam that is in thine own eye? Or how wilt thou say to thy brother, Let me pull out the mote out of thine eye; and behold, a beam is in thine own eye? Thou hypocrite, first cast out the beam out of thine own eye; and then shalt thou see clearly to cast out the mote out of thy brother's eye (Matthew 7:1-5).

He was not excusing sin; He was defining mercy and love. Sin must be dealt with by God and by the overseer of the flock, which is the pastor. If all the saints tried to line everybody up and deal with each other's sin, the church would constantly be in a court of law. This would result in neglect of the great commission in which Jesus told us to go and teach the gospel to those that are lost.

Why can't people truly love one another? Why must there be walls and hypocrisies? Where are the *rivers* of love? Everyone has met those who profess to love Jesus and are considered to be Christians. Yet when they greet you it is with a forced hello, a quick handshake, and a "let's-get-out-of-here" attitude. You know and they know, but they do not think that you know, that you have been a subject of their conversations recently. You sense their insincerity and see the veneer that covers a hypocritical heart.

Their smile does not shine with genuine love. They do not want to be nice, but because of who you are or who you are associated with, they feel it necessary to carry through with the sham. You have done no wrong, but because of your dreams and visions, you become the object of a jealous heart. Instead of choosing to understand and be considerate of you, they choose to twist and misunderstand your motives and plans, because deep down they want you to fall.

They would love to see you tarred and feathered and made a laughingstock or an effigy of hate by the multitudes. Their seething heart of envy, self-love and misguided judgment would love to pass you by, but because you are considered respectable and worthy of knowing, you are extended a handshake and a brief hello just to let you and others know that all is well. It is not well, and no one is fooled, especially Christ!

The person who thinks only of himself, who shouts, complains and insists on his rights in order to make sure he is not forgotten, sooner or later is forgotten, whereas the one who loves and forgets himself is always remembered with love.

Each person chooses whether to be kind or unkind. It is an everyday choice for everyone. It is choosing to do what Jesus said to do in Matthew 7:12, "Therefore all things whatsoever ye would that men should do to you, do ye even so to them: for this is the law and the prophets."

The following prayer was written by Miss Mary Stewart of Washington, D.C., many years ago, and has been adopted by many business and professional women's organizations all over the United States as their official prayer. It is a good prayer for all to adopt:

> Keep us, O God, from pettiness, let us be large in thought, in word, in deed.
>
> Let us be done with fault-finding and leave off self-seeking.
>
> May we put away all pretense and meet each other face to face—without self-pity, and without prejudice.
>
> May we never be hasty in judgment and always generous.
>
> Let us take time for all things; make us to grow calm, serene, and gentle.
>
> Teach us to put into action our better impulses, straight-forward and unafraid.
>
> Grant us to realize it is the little things that create differences, that in the big things of life we are as one.

> And may we strive to touch and know the great, common woman's heart of us all, and, O Lord, let us forget not TO BE KIND. [2]

It is best to carve your name on hearts, and not on marble, wood or stone. This is done by the kind deeds that you do for others. Kind acts are never forgotten by the receiver. Did you know if you made one person happy each day for forty years, that you would have made 14,600 human beings happy and would have lightened their load at least for a little while?

Rev. Purnell Bailey shared the following story to show how this works:

> A convict from Darlington, England, just released from jail, happened to pass Mayor John Morel on the street. Three long years had been spent by the convict in prison for embezzlement and he was sensitive about the social ostracism he expected to get from the people in his home town.
>
> "Hello," greeted the mayor in a cheery tone. "I'm glad to see you! How are you?" The man appeared ill at ease and the discussion stopped.
>
> Years later, according to the story told by J.H. Jowell, Mr. Morel, the mayor, and the released man accidentally

met in another town, and the latter said, "I want to thank you for what you did for me when I came out of prison."

"What did I do?" asked the mayor.

"You spoke a kind word to me and changed my life," replied the grateful man.[3]

This same principle worked for a young man in the city of Philadelphia who worked at a little third-class hotel, in which two tired elderly people entered one night. They went up to the night clerk and pleadingly said, "Mister, please don't tell us you don't have a room. My wife and I have been all over the city looking for a place to stay. We did not know about the big conventions that are here. The hotels at which we usually stay are all full. We're dead tired and it's after midnight. Please don't tell us you don't have a place where we can sleep."

The clerk looked at them a long moment and then told them the hotel was full, but that they could use his room, since he worked all night and would not be occupying it. He said, "I'll be happy for you to be my guests for tonight, even though my room is not as nice as the other rooms."

The next morning at breakfast the elderly couple sent the waiter to get the night clerk, as they had important business to discuss with him. When he approached their table, he recognized them as the couple from the night before. As he sat down they thanked him most sincerely. The husband said, "You are too fine a hotel man to stay in a hotel like this. How would you like for me to build a big, beautiful, luxurious hotel in the city of New York and make you general manager?"

The clerk was astonished and did not know what to say. He wondered at the couple but stammered the words, "It would be wonderful."

His guest then introduced himself. "I'm John Jacob Astor." So the Waldorf Astoria Hotel was built. And the night clerk became, in the years to follow, the best-known hotel man in the world, all because of one act of kindness.

Stephen Grellet, a French-born Quaker who died in New Jersey in 1855, made famous these words: "I shall pass through this world but once. Any good that I can do, or any kindness that I can show to any human being, let me do it now and not defer it. For I shall not pass this way again." [4]

It is not only a grand thing to do good to those you come in contact with, but it is equally important to keep your mouth from speaking evil.

> Remember that charity thinketh no evil, much less repeats it. There are two good rules which ought to be written on every heart: never believe anything bad about anybody

> unless you positively know it is true; never even tell anyone unless you feel that it is absolutely necessary and that God is listening while you tell it. [5]

Love always gives. Whatever you give is what you become, for one retains what he gives. One is known by God and others by how well he loves. John said,

> And this is his commandment, That we should believe on the name of his Son Jesus Christ, and love one another, as he gave us commandment. And he that keepeth his commandments dwelleth in him, and he in him. And hereby we know that he abideth in us, by the Spirit which he hath given us (I John 3:23-24).

Harold Cornelius Sandall said it well in the following poem entitled "Selfishness":

> Love that is hoarded, molds at last.
> Until we know some day,
> The only thing we ever have
> Is what we give away.
>
> And kindness that is never used

But hidden all alone,
Will slowly harden until it is
As hard as any stone.

It is the things we always hold,
That we will lose someday;
The only things we ever keep,
Are what we give away. [6]

A little seven-year-old girl walked into Clay Hall in Beardstown, Illinois, one day in July 1996, during the worst of the Midwest flooding and asked where the people who were sandbagging were. When she was told, "Brick School, five miles north of Beardstown," she said, "Oh, I can't walk that far." She carried a cooler and had heard on the radio that volunteers filling sandbags needed food.

She then asked the man in charge if someone could take her food to the sandbaggers. He assured her that it would be done. She then reached into the cooler and handed him two bananas, a can of pork and beans, three cans of soda, a grapefruit, and five Tootsie Rolls. Then she walked out the door carrying an empty cooler. No name, no address, just a happy little heart because she gave what she could.

Love is not stingy; it always has room for just one more. Love is a miracle worker that takes a little bit and multiplies it into a whole lot. It manifests itself not by grabbing but by releasing. It says, "What I have is yours," and then proceeds to share. It sets the soul free from sordidness and greed.

Love is a liberator. Perfect love casts out fear. Hate, violence and vengeance are all forms of fear. Fear that someone will get ahead of you on the ladder of success causes envy and hate. Hate breeds violence. John said again, "There is no fear in love; but perfect love casteth out fear: because fear hath torment. He that feareth is not made perfect in love" (I John 4:18).

Love is very unselfish, for one who loves cannot calculate. Love does not keep track of, "I did this and this, now you owe me this." Love is giving away, expecting nothing in return. Paul wrote in Romans to "Owe no one anything, but to love one another: for he that loveth another hath fulfilled the law" (Romans 13:8). Our duty is to be in the debt of love to each other. Love is the only thing that one is allowed to be in debt to; not only are we allowed, but we are encouraged to be so.

Steven Mosley, in his book *A Tale of Three Virtues*, tells of the terrible news about a car accident that killed several members of Madge Harrah's family. The news came as she, her husband and children were preparing to move to another state.

The house was in chaos. Madge had to fight through her grief to get ready—find the right clothes for the kids in all the boxes, get tickets to fly home so she could be with her mother, and check on details about the funeral. As she was walking around the house in a daze, aimlessly picking things up and putting them down, the doorbell rang. It was a neighbor. What on earth could he want?

"I've come to clean your shoes," he said simply.

Madge didn't understand. As she stared, the neighbor explained, "When my father died, it took me hours to get the children's shoes cleaned and shined for the funeral. So that's what I've come to do for you."

The neighbor settled himself on the kitchen floor and scraped and washed and shined all the shoes in the house. Watching him concentrate quietly on his task helped Madge pull her thoughts together and begin her own preparations. Later, when she returned from the laundry room, the neighbor was gone. But lined neatly against the wall stood all the shoes, spotless and gleaming. [7]

Quiet, unassuming love had been at work. It was being kind to someone in need, doing something instead of saying, "Call me if you need me." Someone once said, "Love can be measured by the sacrifice it makes."

Max Lucado shares in his book, *No Wonder They Call Him the Saviour*, a touching story of true love.

> Maria's husband died when she was a young girl with a little baby called Christina. They lived in a small house in the poor neighborhood on the outskirts of a Brazilian village. As Christina grew older, she seemed discontent and spoke often of going to the city. She dreamed of trading her dusty neighborhood for exciting avenues and city life.
>
> Her mother often warned her of the danger for a young girl alone in the city. But one morning Maria woke up to find her daughter's bed empty. The mother gathered up all her money and ran out of the house down to a local drugstore to get some pictures made of herself. With her purse full of pictures of herself, she boarded the next bus to Rio de Janeiro.
>
> Maria knew Christina had no way of earning money, and she also knew that she was stubborn. When pride meets hunger, a human will do things that were before

unthinkable. Knowing this, Maria began her search—bars, hotels, nightclubs, any place with the reputation for street walkers. She went to them all. And at each place she left her picture—taped on a bathroom mirror, tacked to a hotel bulletin board, fastened to a corner phone booth. And on the back of each photo she wrote a note. It wasn't long until both the money and the pictures ran out, and Maria had to go home. The weary mother wept as the bus began its long journey back to her small village.

It was a few weeks later that young Christina descended the hotel stairs. Her young face was tired. Her brown eyes no longer danced with youth but spoke of pain and fear. Her laughter was broken. Her dream had become a nightmare.

As she reached the bottom of the stairs, her eyes noticed a familiar face. She looked again, and there on the lobby mirror was a small picture of her mother. Christina's eyes burned and her throat tightened as she walked across the room and removed the small photo. Written on the back was this compelling invitation, "Whatever you have done, whatever you have become, it doesn't matter. Please come home."

She did. [8]

This is true love. Unconditional love. Love that does not demand its own way, but loves in spite of hurts afflicted. The Apostle Paul described love as thinking no evil, bearing all things, enduring all things and summing it up with the immortal words, "Charity never faileth" (I Corinthians 13:8). Love just never gives up.

Love is never wasted. An act of love is always given back in an overflowing amount, pressed down and shaken together. Love is the signpost to the world that Jesus is a part of a person's life. The infilling of His Spirit inside of man is manifested by the love shown to others.

When Jesus was dealing with the subject of the true vine and the branches in John 15, He spoke often of loving one another. In the first 17 verses, Jesus explicitly said three times to love one another. It was not just a casual comment, but it was a commandment. "This is my commandment, That ye love one another, as I have loved you" (John 15:12). He ended the discourse with, "These things I command you, that ye love one another" (John 15:17).

Tertullian once wrote about the contrast between the early century Christians and unbelievers: "'See,' say they, 'how they love each other'; for they themselves hate each other: and 'see how ready they are to die for each other'; for they themselves are more ready to slay each other." [9]

As the world grows darker with hate, evil, disrespect and murderous deeds, so should the church grow brighter with true love, respect, honor and kindness. Then the world will know the true disciples of Christ!

Four:

Kindness is Being Gentle

Gentleness is sensed by others. The gleam of the eye can often show forth a gentle spirit. Brian Cavanaugh proves this in the following story which appeared in *The Sower's Seeds:*

It was a bitter cold evening in northern Virginia many years ago. The old man's beard was glazed by winter's frost while he waited for a ride across the river. The wait seemed endless. His body became numb and stiff from the frigid north wind.

He heard the faint, steady rhythm of approaching hooves galloping along the frozen path. Anxiously, he watched as several horsemen rounded the bend. He let the first one pass by without an effort to get his attention. Then another passed by, and another. Finally, the last rider neared the spot where the old man caught the rider's eye and said, "Sir, would you mind giving an old man a ride to the other side? There doesn't appear to be a passageway by foot."

Reining his horse, the rider replied, "Sure thing. Hop aboard." Seeing the old man was unable to lift his half-frozen body from the ground, the horseman dismounted and helped the old man onto the horse. The horseman took the old man not just across the river, but to his destination, which was just a few miles away.

As they neared the tiny but cozy cottage, the horseman's curiosity caused him to inquire, "Sir, I notice that you let several other riders pass by without making an effort to secure a ride. Then I came up and you immediately asked me for a ride. I'm curious why, on such a bitter winter night, you would wait and ask the last rider. What if I had refused and left you there?"

The old man lowered himself slowly down from the horse, looked the rider straight in the eyes, and replied, "I've been around these here parts for some time. I reckon I know people pretty good." The old-timer continued, "I looked into the eyes of the other riders and immediately saw there was no concern for my situation. It would have been useless even to ask them for a ride. But when I looked into your eyes, kindness and compassion were evident. I knew, then and there, that your gentle spirit would welcome the opportunity to give me assistance in my time of need."

Those heartwarming comments touched the horseman deeply. "I'm most grateful for what you have said," he told the old man. "May I never get too busy in my own affairs that I fail to respond to the needs of others with kindness and compassion."

With that, Thomas Jefferson turned his horse around and made his way back to the White House.

This chapter will address the subject of gentleness and seek to show that it is important for a person to possess a gentle spirit, and that the Lord requires it. In order to prove a positive quality, often it is needful to discuss that which is its opposite. The scripture does this in II Timothy 2:24: "And the servant of the Lord must not strive; but be gentle unto all men."

"It is an honour for a man to cease from strife: but every fool will be meddling" (Proverbs 20:3). What is strife? It is exertion or contention for superiority; it is emulation, which is ambitious or envious rivalry. Being contentious and envious always leaves a person with an IOU, holding the bag, and owing someone something. One does not win through strife; one only loses.

James the Apostle wrote under the inspiration of the Holy Spirit about envy and strife.

> But if ye have bitter envying and strife in your hearts, glory not, and lie not against the truth. This wisdom descendeth not from above, but is earthly, sensual, devilish. For where envying and strife is, there is confusion and every evil work. But the wisdom that is from above is first pure, then peaceable, *gentle* and easy to be intreated, full of mercy and good fruits, without partiality, and without hypocrisy (James 3:14-17).

Envy is sensual and devilish, resulting in confusion and evil. This does not sound like a background for success, only failure. What would cause anyone to play around with such spirits when they are so demeaning? Is it not better to put on Christ and show forth His love and gentleness by helping each other to become successful, and genuinely rejoicing when someone else does something well? Everyone is blessed and grows in that type of atmosphere. It is the true way to show forth Christ.

J. R. Miller wrote,

> All human hearts hunger for tenderness. We are made for love—not only to love, but to be loved. Harshness pains us. Ungentleness touches our sensitive spirits as frost touches the flowers. It stunts the growth of all lovely things. Gentleness is like a genial summer to our life. Beneath its warm, nourishing influence beautiful things in us grow.
>
> There are many people who have a special need for tenderness. We cannot know what secret burdens many of those about us are carrying, what hidden griefs burn like fires in the hearts of those with whom we mingle in our common life. Not all grief wears the outward garb of mourning; sunny faces ofttimes veil heavy hearts. Many people who make no audible appeal for sympathy yet crave tenderness—they certainly need it, though they ask it not—as they bow beneath their burden. There is no weakness in such a yearning. We remember how our Master Himself longed for expressions of love when He was passing through His deepest experiences of suffering, and

how bitterly He was disappointed when His friends failed Him.

We can never do amiss in showing gentleness. There is no day when it will be untimely; there is no place where it will not find welcome. It will harm no one, and it may save someone from despair.

The Proverbs speak much about the wrathful or striving man. "A wrathful man stirreth up strife; but he that is slow to anger appeaseth strife" (Proverbs 15:18). This is the secret to staying the hand of strife. Learn to hold on to your temper and be a peacemaker instead of blowing resentful steam in everyone's faces.

The one who stirs up strife is not always loud, boisterous and full of temper, but sometimes whispers. Proverbs 16:28 says, "A froward man soweth strife; and a whisperer separateth chief friends." It starts as a little thing, and the more one talks the bigger it becomes. Solomon described it well in Proverbs 17:14 which says, "The beginning of strife is as when one letteth out water; therefore leave off contention, before it be meddled with."

In other words, keep your mouth closed. "Where no wood is, there the fire goeth out; so where there is no talebearer, the strife ceaseth" (Proverbs 26:20). Quit stirring things up; let them die down. Pray about it as much as you talk about it, and something good will be brought out of it.

The contentious are continually stirring up things. They love to tell some juicy piece of gossip about someone else. It feeds their ego and, "As coals are to burning coals, and wood to fire; so is a contentious man to kindle strife" (Proverbs 26:21). The person filled with fiery contention is just waiting to burn someone through envy and strife.

The bottom line of strife is pride. It is the opposite of humility. True humbleness of mind does not like to see other people hurt, but a proud heart gets a kick out of seeing someone topple and fall. The scripture says, "He that is of a proud heart stirreth up strife; but he that putteth his trust in the Lord shall be made fat" (Proverbs 28:25). In other words, the one who trusts shall be blessed, but the agitator shall be brought low.

Paul couples strife with the sin of drunkenness. He wrote, "Let us walk honestly, as in the day; not in rioting and drunkenness, not in chambering and wantonness, not in strife and envying" (Romans 13:13). It is the carnal person who is full of strife. He is full of his own self, instead of the Holy Spirit of God.

Paul wrote, "For ye are yet carnal: for whereas there is among you envying and strife; and divisions, are ye not carnal...?" (I Corinthians 3:3). He was telling them that they were arguing about things that should not even be discussed, that their arguments were foolish, unfounded and not pleasing to God.

The way of Christ is to prefer the other person, not always pushing self in front. Paul expressed it like this:

> Let nothing be done through strife or vainglory; but in lowliness of mind let each esteem other better than themselves. Look not every man on his own things, but every man also on the things of others (Philippians 2:3-4).

This certainly knocks gossip and contention out of a person's conversation.

Mark someone who is continually putting down other people or spreading dirt about others. Paul said it, "Now I beseech you, brethren, mark them which cause divisions and offences contrary to the doctrine which ye have learned: and avoid them" (Romans 16:17).

One of the greatest doctrines Jesus dealt with was how to treat one another. He emphasized over and over that love was the theme of His gospel. It is interesting to note that in Matthew 5, He coupled perfection with knowing how to treat people. He said,

> Ye have heard that it hath been said, Thou shalt love thy neighbour, and hate thine enemy. But I say unto you, Love your enemies, bless them that curse you, do good to them that hate you, and pray for them which despitefully use you, and persecute you; That ye may be the children of your Father which is in heaven: for he maketh his sun to rise on the evil and on the good, and sendeth rain on the just and on the unjust. For if ye love them which love you, what reward have ye? do not even the publicans the same? And if ye salute your brethren only, what do ye more than others? do not even the publicans so? Be ye therefore perfect, even as your Father which is in heaven is perfect (Matthew 5:43-48).

What is He talking about here? He is talking about the higher love that is not available on the earth. This kind of love identifies one with Christ. Just as the man who causes divisions is to be marked, so is the man who loves as Christ loves. Solomon wrote, "Mark the perfect man, and behold the upright; for the end of that man is peace" (Proverbs 37:37).

"We must overcome our enemies by gentleness, win them over by forbearance. Let us not at once wither the big tree from which a more skillful gardener may yet entice fruit." [1]

Gentleness is the mark of someone who has been through trials and learned the lessons from them. He has been made gentle by the hand of the Master. Instead of continual striving, he has learned—sometimes the hard way—that it is best to be gentle.

Walter B. Knight once told the story of how Dwight Moody and Ira Sankey many years ago were traveling in a railway coach, going west. A drunk man recognized Moody. He had heard him preach, and began to mimic him. Moody became angry and demanded that the conductor do something about it. The conductor spoke kindly to the man, helped him to a seat, sat beside him and talked calmly to him. Presently the drunk man was sound asleep. Moody sat thinking about what had occurred and conviction settled upon him when he thought of his hastily spoken words and un-Christlike attitude. He said to Sankey, "Last night I preached on the Good Samaritan, and here I find that my feet are in the shoes of the priest and the Levite. I have missed a chance to practice what I preached last night."

The opposite of being gentle is having a fierce attitude, referred to in II Timothy 3:1-3.

> This know also, that in the last days perilous times shall come. For men shall be lovers of their own selves, covet-

ous, boasters, proud, blasphemers, disobedient to parents, unthankful, unholy, without natural affection, trucebreakers, false accusers, incontinent, *FIERCE*, despisers of those that are good.

A fierce person bristles with arguments and self-defense, showing no meekness. He shouts in tones of anger and pierces the very soul of the receiver. C.A. Lufburrow said it well in his poem entitled, "The Echo."

I shouted aloud and louder
While out on the plain one day;
The sound grew faint and fainter
Until it had died away.
My words had gone forever,
They left no trace or track.
But the hills nearby caught up the cry
And sent an echo back.

I spoke a word in anger
To one who was my friend,
Like a knife it cut him deeply,
A wound that was hard to mend.
That word, so thoughtlessly uttered,

I would we could both forget,
But its echo lives and memory gives
The recollection yet.

How many hearts are broken,
How many friends are lost
By some unkind word spoken
Before we count the cost!
But a word or deed of kindness
Will repay a hundredfold,
For it echoes again in the hearts of men
And carries a joy untold. [2]

"Speak kind words and you will hear kind echoes" (Bahn).

One of my favorite stories, *A Sandpiper to Bring You Joy,* written by Mary Sherman Hilbert, relates the pain of a woman who realized too late that her harshness could never be retracted. Regret could never bring back the moment in time that she chose to be harsh instead of gentle.

Several years ago, a neighbor related to me an experience that happened to her one winter on a beach in Washington State. The incident stuck in my mind and I took note of what she said. Later, at a writers' conference, the conversation came back to me and I felt I had to set it down. Here is her story, as haunting to me now as when I first heard it:

She was six years old when I first met her on the beach near where I live. I drive to this beach, a distance of three or four miles, whenever the world begins to close in on me.

She was building a sand castle or something and looked up, her eyes as blue as the sea.

"Hello," she said. I answered with a nod, not really in the mood to bother with a small child.

"I'm building," she said.

"I see that. What is it?" I asked, not caring.

"Oh, I don't know. I just like the feel of the sand."

That sounds good, I thought, and slipped off my shoes. A sandpiper glided by.

"That's a joy," the child said.

"It's what?"

"It's a joy. My mama says sandpipers come to bring us joy."

The bird went glissading down the beach. "Good-bye, joy," I muttered to myself, "hello, pain," and turned to walk on. I was depressed; my life seemed completely out of balance.

"What's your name?" She wouldn't give up.

"Ruth," I answered. "I'm Ruth Peterson."

"Mine's Windy." It sounded like Windy. "And I'm six."

"Hi, Windy."

She giggled. "You're funny," she said. In spite of my gloom I laughed too and walked on.

Her musical giggle followed me. "Come again, Mrs. P," she called. "We'll have another happy day."

The days and weeks that followed belonged to others: a group of unruly Boy Scouts, PTA meetings, an ailing mother.

The sun was shining one morning as I took my hands out of the dishwater. "I need a sandpiper," I said to myself, gathering up my coat.

The never-changing balm of the seashore awaited me. The breeze was chilly, but I strode along, trying to recapture the serenity I needed. I had forgotten the child and was startled when she appeared.

"Hello, Mrs. P," she said. "Do you want to play?"

"What did you have in mind?" I asked, with a twinge of annoyance.

"I don't know. You say."

"How about charades?" I asked sarcastically.

The tinkling laughter burst forth again. "I don't know what that is."

"Then let's just walk." Looking at her, I noticed the delicate fairness of her face.

"Where do you live?" I asked.

"Over there." She pointed toward a row of summer cottages. Strange, I thought in winter.

"Where do you go to school?"

"I don't go to school. Mommy says we're on vacation."

She chattered little-girl talk as we strolled up the beach, but my mind was on other things. When I left for home, Windy said it had been a happy day. Feeling surprisingly better, I smiled at her and agreed.

Three weeks later, I rushed to my beach in a state of near panic. I was in no mood even to greet Windy. I thought I saw her mother on the porch and felt like demanding she keep her child at home.

"Look, if you don't mind," I said crossly when Windy caught up with me, "I'd rather be alone today." She seemed unusually pale and out of breath.

"Why?" she asked.

I turned on her and shouted, "Because my mother died!"—and thought, my God, why was I saying this to a little child?

"Oh," she said quietly, "then this is a bad day."

"Yes, and yesterday and the day before that and—oh, go away!"

"Did it hurt?"

"Did what hurt?" I was exasperated with her, with myself.

"When she died?"

"Of course it hurt!" I snapped, misunderstanding. Wrapped up in myself, I strode off.

A month or so after that, when I next went to the beach, she wasn't there. Feeling guilty, ashamed and admitting to myself I missed her, I went up to the cottage after my walk and knocked at the door. A drawn-looking young woman with honey-colored hair opened the door.

"Hello," I said. "I'm Ruth Peterson. I missed your little girl today and wondered where she was."

"Oh yes, Mrs. Peterson, please come in.

"Wendy talked of you so much. I'm afraid I allowed her to bother you. If she was a nuisance, please accept my apologies."

"Not at all—she's a delightful child," I said, suddenly realizing I meant it. "Where is she?"

"Wendy died last week, Mrs. Peterson. She had leukemia. Maybe she didn't tell you."

Struck dumb, I groped for a chair. My breath caught.

"She loved this beach; so when she asked to come, we couldn't say no. She seemed so much better here and had a lot of what she called happy days. But the last few weeks she declined rapidly...." Her voice faltered. "She left something for you...if only I can find it. Could you wait a moment while I look?"

I nodded stupidly, my mind racing for something, anything, to say to this lovely young woman.

She handed me a smeared envelope, with MRS. P printed in bold, childish letters.

Inside was a drawing in bright crayon hues—a yellow beach, a blue sea, a brown bird. Underneath was carefully printed:

A SANDPIPER TO BRING YOU JOY

Tears welled up in my eyes, and a heart that had almost forgotten how to love opened wide. I took Wendy's mother in my arms. “I’m sorry, I’m sorry, I’m so sorry,” I muttered over and over, and we wept together.

The precious little picture is framed now and hangs in my study. Six words—one for each year of her life—that speak to me of inner harmony, courage, undemanding love. A gift from a child with sea-blue eyes and hair the color of sand—who taught me the gift of love. [3]

Five:

Kindness is Being Respectful and Courteous

It is best to be respectful all the time to all people, for one does not always know to whom he is speaking until it is too late, as is proven in the following story:

One Sunday a scholarly-looking man, plainly dressed, went into a church in Holland and took a seat near the pulpit. In a few minutes a lady approached the pew, and seeing the stranger in it curtly asked him to leave. He took one of the seats reserved for the poor, and joined devoutly in the service.

When the service was over, one of the woman's friends asked her if she knew who it was whom she had ordered out of her seat. "No," she replied, "but it was only some stranger, I suppose."

"It was King Oscar of Sweden," replied her informant. "He is here visiting the queen."

Kindness is a mark of the well-bred. It reveals itself at all times and under all circumstances. [1]

Washington Irving wrote, "The constant interchange of those thousand little courtesies which imperceptibly sweeten life has a happy effect upon the features, and spreads a mellow evening charm over the wrinkles of old age." [2]

Courtesies not only benefit the one receiving them, but they do something beautiful for their giver. Several years ago during a Courtesy Campaign sponsored by the Advertising and Sales Executive Club of Kansas City, one thousand silver dollars were flown in from Denver. For one week "mystery shoppers" visited all types of stores, banks and other places of business. They listened to telephone operators, and observed bus and street car drivers. Each day they made a written report regarding persons they found most courteous. Each one so designated received a silver dollar and card of congratulations with a "courtesy pays" button. The fifteen outstandingly polite people were to be guests at a banquet and receive $25 each.

Every day the Lord keeps silent record of whether His children are courteous or not. A story that warms the heart, written by Elaine Pondant, appeared in the March 1994 issue of *Reader's Digest.* It was a simple story about a bed that had been given to Elaine by her mother. One day Elaine decided that she would sand it down and refinish it because it had some scratches on it. So she collected all the materials she needed to do this, but just before she started, she noticed that one of the scratches was a date.

This caught her eye and she was curious about it. Then she remembered: that was the day her mother and father had been married. She started looking for other dates. She found, "Elizabeth, October 22, 1947," and then she found, "Sam, June 8, 1959." Curious as to what these two dates represented, she called her mother on the telephone and inquired. She said, "Mom, there are a lot of dates and names I don't recognize on the headboard. Who is Elizabeth?"

"She's your sister," Mom answered.

Elaine knew her mother had lost a baby, but she never thought it was that important. She asked, "You gave her a name?"

"Yes," her mother replied. "Elizabeth has been watching us from heaven for 45 years."

Elaine then asked her mother about the date June 8, 1959, which had "Sam" written by it.

"Sam was a black man who worked for your father at the plant," answered her mother. "Your father was fair with everyone, treating those under him with equal respect, no matter what their race or religion. But there was a lot of racial tension at that time. There was also a union strike and a lot of trouble.

"One night some strikers surrounded your dad before he got to his car. Sam showed up with several friends, and the crowd dispersed. No one was hurt. The strike eventually ended, but your dad never forgot Sam. He said Sam was an answer to his prayers." [3]

The kindness shown by Sam to Elaine's father paid off—it kept him from being hurt and may have saved his life.

Respect is considering another worthy of esteem. It is giving someone regard, consideration and honor. It is respecting someone's opinion and not cutting him off because of his culture, color or background. It is respecting a person in spite of his limitations, accepting him as a friend and person even if he has disabilities or is considered different than others.

Lee Elliott's article entitled, "My Most Unforgettable Character," which appeared in the same *Reader's Digest* mentioned above, exemplifies this. He shares his first encounter with John Van Berkel. It was at freshman-orientation day at El Camino High School in Sacramento, California. John stood apart from the other students. His arms and legs seemed too long. Homely and awkward, wearing thick glasses, he hunched his shoulders as if to hide his phenomenal height.

When Lee Elliot, the teacher, saw him, he tried to put him at ease by saying, “Well, students, I see our future basketball star.” Then he smiled at John, trying to put him at ease. Then he said he committed the blunder that most people make when they meet someone who is different. He asked, “Just how tall are you?”

“I’m five-foot-twenty-two and growing,” John answered with an impish grin. Translation: six feet, ten inches. “By the way,” he added, “have you ever heard anyone ask, ‘Just how fat are you?’”

Lee reflected back over John’s life, sharing the details. He had Marfan’s syndrome. Marfan’s weakens and loosens connective tissue, producing the classic symptoms of extreme tallness, nearsightedness, abnormally long fingers and an enlarged aorta. John became part of the school system, but not as Lee originally thought. His disease kept him from being a basketball star, but it did not keep him from reading. He constantly had a book which was held just inches from his face because of his poor eyesight.

John found his place in the drama department, moving scenery, working backstage with lights and sound equipment, and keeping everyone in stitches. In spite of his disease he had a keen sense of humor and seemed to live life to the fullest. One night during a complex technical production, John kept missing lighting cues. When Lee lost patience and yelled at him, he stalked off. Backstage, he said to Lee through clenched teeth, "Don't you understand? I can't see!"

Lee explained his own feelings. "Of course, I thought, ashamed. With his thick glasses, John was still able to get around and even read, but his eyesight may have been poor enough to get him classified as legally blind. I realized how often I'd taken advantage of his time and energy without thanking him. The next day, I bought a magnifying glass and a high-intensity lamp to attach to the light board. Then I vowed never again to take John—or anyone else—for granted." [4]

Why should only the normal, rich or beautiful be respected? It is a sin to show respect of persons. Everyone deserves respect. The Apostle James gives a whole chapter to this subject, capping it with this scripture, "But if ye have respect to persons, ye commit sin, and are convinced of the law as transgressors" (James 2:9).

There are levels of authority that require great respect, and respect should be shown to them. But that does not mean that those who are not important should not be respected. For instance, if an elderly person walked into a living room full of children who were seated in every available chair, it would be disrespectful of the children to not get up and give the elder a chair. The respect shown to the elder, who deserved to be seated because of his age and experience, did not take away from the respect the elder should show the child. The elder should extend thanks back with a twinkle in the eye and a smile on his face and acknowledge the gesture of respect shown him by simply saying thank you in return.

Respect is loving someone the way he is, even if he is not like you. Of course, there are exceptions to every rule. How can one respect a murderer, child molester, or the like? The respect discussed in this book deals with loving God first and secondly loving your neighbor as yourself, principles on which the whole law hinges. When a lawyer asked Jesus a question, tempting him, and saying, "Master, which is the great commandment in the law?" Jesus said unto him,

> ...Thou shalt love the Lord thy God with all thy heart, and with all thy soul, and with all thy mind. This is the first and great commandment. And the second is like unto it, Thou shalt love thy neighbor as thyself. On these two commandments hang all the law and the prophets (Matthew 22:37-40).

Something has happened to our world because these two commandments have been violated. An article by Helen Gibson from Preston, England, appeared in the November 1993 issue of *Time* magazine. It describes part of the courtroom drama associated with the two ten-year-old boys who murdered two-year-old James Bulger in Liverpool in February of that year. She wrote,

> The defendants, sitting beside two social workers, listen with pale and expressionless faces. Both come from broken homes, with parents reported to have alcohol problems. While Boy B's parents have both been in court, sometimes crying as the grisly murder was described, neither A's mother nor his father has attended the trial. Boy A has kept his composure for the most part, but his companion has sobbed and clutched at the social worker beside him. [5]

This story is a terrible reflection of the condition of our world. John Leo, in his article, "Watching 'As the Jury Turns,'" which appeared in *U.S. News & World Report* February 14, 1994, predicts another terrible onslaught of crime. He reports,

We are deep into the era of the abuse excuse. The doctrine of victimology—claiming victim status means you are not responsible for your actions—is beginning to warp the legal system. "Get ready for a huge burst of criminal defenses based on abuse," says Allan Campo, a litigation analyst in Lafayette, La., whose firm helps prepare lawyers for trial. "In about 10 years, the public will be bored with it, but that will be after a lot of murderers get off."

A movement that began with the slogan, *Don't blame the victim*, now strives to blame murder victims for their own deaths. Virginia Postrel, the editor of *Reason* magazine, writes, "We have created a culture of excuse, and it has conquered our courtrooms." It isn't just victimology. Part of the problem is that one of the central thinkings of American pop psychology—feeling is more important than thinking—has also penetrated the culture. [6]

This article appeared in conjunction with the 1994 skating scandal. Just a short time before the Olympic Games were scheduled to open in Lillehammer, Norway, Nancy Kerrigan, a figure skater scheduled to be in the Olympic quest, was clubbed on the knee. It was a sordid script written into the lives of two skaters who wanted to be first. Because one thought maybe there was a possibility of her not being first, plans were made to disable the other. Jeff Gillooly, Tonya Harding's ex-husband, and Shawn Eckardt, Harding's bodyguard, hatched up the plan after Harding returned from a competition in Japan. She was disgruntled over a judging that she felt was biased toward rival Kerrigan.

It is reported that Eckardt first suggested to Gillooly that they, with a threat, just frighten Kerrigan out of competing, but the scheme quickly snowballed into the ugly plot to bash Kerrigan's jumping leg. Eckardt enlisted the services of Derrick Smith and Shane Stant, petty criminals living in Arizona, who at first named a fee between $65,000 and $100,000 to do the deed. In the end Smith and Stant attacked Kerrigan for less than $5,000, in the hope that if Harding won a gold medal at the Olympics, they would become *World Bodyguard Service* to the stars. Gillooly maintains that Harding knew about their plans almost from the start.

The public is constantly bombarded with stories that reflect the loss of respect for one another, and it seems that one just emerges from one shocking story only to be knocked down by another. The old-fashioned respect and regard for honesty seems to be replaced with, "Whatever it takes to win, do it."

This disregard for one another is found in every level of communication. It is found among youth as well as professional athletes. Charles Krauthammer shares some horrendously awful information on "The Scourge of Illegitimacy" in the *Washington Post.* He writes,

> "Sex Codes Among Inner-City Youth" is the title of a remarkable five-year study by University of Pennsylvania Professor Elijah Anderson, a scrupulous and sympathetic observer of ghetto life. He describes in excruciating detail the sex and abandonment "game" played by boys and girls in a blighted Philadelphia community. It is the story of family breakdown on an unprecedented scale.
>
> Casual sex with as many women as possible, impregnating one or more, and getting them to "have your baby" brings a boy the ultimate in esteem from his peers and makes him a man. But because owning up to a pregnancy goes against the peer-group ethic of "hit and run," abandonment is the norm. The results: illegitimacy rates of up to 80 percent, intergenerational poverty, social chaos. [7]

The purpose of this book is not to list all the terrible things that are now taking place, but rather to be a call to arms. It is time to do what you can. If no one does anything at all, we will all die under the modern-day scourge of sin and disrespect for one another and the finer values of life. It is time to get back to God and His principles.

There are still those who retain old-fashioned care and respect for their fellow man.

> New York City subway conductor Harry Nugent transformed his train with colorful announcements which brought smiles to weary travelers. After twenty years of service, two publishers are offering him book contracts that talk about how to get from Point A to Point B. Or, as he liked to announce when his train was stuck or delayed, "Someone once said that success is a journey and not a destination, and by that definition we're eminently successful."
>
> Nugent's unusual approach to his work has drawn accolades from the city and the Municipal Arts Society, but his biggest fans were the people who rode with him. Even those with glum faces could not help cracking a smile. "He made such a difference," says Peggy Barber, who went out of her way to take Nugent's subway. "People got off his train and they weren't pushing and shoving. They were smiling." [8]

What if *everyone* started caring like Harry Nugent cared? He did not know some of the people, but he treated them all with respect and passed along something that enriched their life. People scrambled to get on his train because it was a bright spot in a dark day.

A journey of a thousand miles begins with the first step. It may be too late to respect some people, but it is never too late to change, for today is the first day of the rest of your life. If you are in the habit of running roughshod over people or treating them shabbily, that habit can be broken, though it will take some effort. First of all, pray to the Lord God and ask Him to show you how to love and respect, and let His Word become a part of your daily life: it is a light. Then make a conscious effort to be respectful and kind. Everyone should seek to be respectful and courteous to others. No one is too big or too little to disregard being kind and considerate towards another.

George Washington proved this truth. Once he was riding across the farmlands with a company of gentlemen, when the last horse jumped over a stone fence and knocked over a number of stones, leaving a large opening. Washington suggested that they stop and repair it, but the others shrugged their shoulders, so he said nothing more and rode on with them.

When the party disbanded, one of them, riding homeward, found Washington back in the farmer's fence, carefully replacing the stones. "Oh, General," chattered the man, "You are too big a man to be doing a thing like that."

"No," answered Washington, gravely inspecting his work, "I'm just the right size." Washington was preaching his sermon in the universal language of action. Words would have bored the farmer no end, but that deed of neighborliness spoke for itself. [9]

Peter gave instructions as to proper behavior on the part of a believer.

> Finally, be ye all of one mind, having compassion one of another, love as brethren, be pitiful, be courteous: Not rendering evil for evil, or railing for railing: but contrariwise blessing; knowing that ye are thereunto called, that ye should inherit a blessing. For he that will love life, and see good days, let him refrain his tongue from evil, and his lips that they speak no guile (I Peter 3:8-10).

Courtesy, as shown here, is associated with how one person talks to another. There is no justifiable excuse for giving a person a good tongue-lashing, even when he deserves it.

Courtesy is the language of gentlemen and gentlewomen. It costs nothing but pays well. A person that speaks a blessing in a courteous manner is promised a blessing as well.

Horace Mann said well, "Manners easily and rapidly mature into morals." What you are is what you become. If you ride roughshod over others then you will become a shoddy person inside. If your tongue speaks evil then you will be filled with evil feelings. If you stare at a person coldly without giving him a smile, then you are even colder on the inside.

The Apostle Paul wrote, "Be not deceived: evil communications corrupt good manners" (I Corinthians 15:33). A person communicates by speech, body language and mannerisms. It is important to guard that which would corrupt or enhance. The art of communication is a treasure that needs to be handled wisely and guarded closely, for it influences manners. Then manners develop into morals, that which a person becomes on the inside.

William Ewart Gladstone, Chancellor of the Exchequer in Britain, showed true courtesy and thoughtfulness even when he had a right to do otherwise. He sent down to the Treasury for information containing certain statistics upon which to base his budget proposals. The statistician made a mistake, but Gladstone was not aware of it. Gladstone did not take the time to verify the figures, being fully confident of the man's ability because of the man's previous record.

He went before the House of Commons and made his speech, basing his appeal on the incorrect figures that had been given him. His speech, when placed in the newspaper, exposed its glaring inaccuracies. Mr. Gladstone went to his office overwhelmed with embarrassment and sent for the statistician who came trembling with fear. Imagine his surprise when Mr. Gladstone told him that he wanted to thank him for what had happened. He said, "I know how much you must be disturbed over what has happened, and I have sent for you to put you at your ease. For a long time you have been engaged in handling the intricacies of the national accounts, and this is the first mistake you have made. I want to congratulate you, and express to you my keen appreciation." [10]

One successful executive shared his keen awareness of taking into consideration what other people felt. He said, "I imagine myself as the person who will be sitting there, and see what I would be feeling, thinking and wanting if I were them. What questions would I have? What would be my concerns? I then figure out how best to respond. I prepare for all important meetings by trying to fully understand the concerns of everyone there."

A person shows what kind of a person he is by how he treats other people. The Ten Commandments of Human Relations have been passed down from generation to generation. The worn-out copy I have says the author is unknown, but the content is excellent and simply says:

1. Speak to people. There is nothing as nice as a cheerful word of greeting.
2. Smile at people. It takes 72 muscles to frown: 14 to smile.
3. Call people by name. The sweetest music is the sound of their own name.
4. Be friendly and helpful.
5. Be cordial. Speak and act as if everything you do is a genuine pleasure.
6. Be genuinely interested in people. You can like most everybody if you try.
7. Be generous with praise—cautious with criticism.
8. Be considerate of the feelings of others. It will be appreciated.
9. Be thoughtful of the opinions of others. There are three sides to a controversy—yours, the other fellow's, and the right one.

10. Be alert to give service. What counts most in life is what we do for others.

This has proven to work successfully many times over. It worked many years ago for a poor boy who was an apprentice at a shop. For several years he passed a certain store every morning as the neighboring church clock struck six. At that particular time a very precise old merchant always took down the shutters of his store. The boy and merchant bowed to one another, each saying, "Good morning, sir." Imagine the boy's surprise when he learned that the old gentleman had suddenly died, and left him his whole business and stock.

It is time to be kind, show respect and walk a mile in another's moccasins before criticizing him. *The King's Highway* printed an interesting feature entitled, "Have You Ever Noticed?"

> When the other fellow acts that way, he is *ugly*; when you do, it is *nerves*.
>
> When the other fellow is set in his ways, he is *obstinate*; when you are, it is just *firmness*.
>
> When the other fellow does not like your friend, he is *prejudiced*; when you do not like his, you simply are showing that you are a *good judge* of human nature.

When the other fellow takes time to do things, he is *dead slow*; when you do, you are *deliberate.*

When the other fellow spends a lot, he is *spendthrift;* when you do, you are *generous.*

When the other fellow picks flaws in things, he is *cranky;* when you do, you are *discriminating.*

When the other fellow is mild in his manners, he is *weak;* when you are, you are being *gracious.*

When the other fellow gets destructive, he is *tough;* when you do, you are *forceful.* [11]

Six:

Kindness is Showing Honor

In the book, *A Tale of Three Virtues*, Steven Mosley describes how honor and humility work together. He writes,

> John defines love as God sending his Son as an atoning sacrifice for our sins. His blood covers a world full of terrible transgressions. Hard honor begins from this point; it's the love that covers a multitude of sins, sweeping away the garbage.
>
> Hard honor is immensely useful as a clearing agent. It eliminates all kinds of conditions and expectations that people huffing and puffing indignantly erect as barriers. Just as light humility gets us past all the useless baggage

> an insecure ego can pile up inside us, so hard honor gets us past all the petty faults that can hang us up in relating to others. [1]

A humble, kind spirit overlooks glaring faults. It allows the other person to feel bathed in the glow of candlelight instead of exposed in the bright beam of a searchlight. It sees people through the eyes and spirit of Jesus. The potential is seen, not just the defect.

Where there is true honor and kindness, the needs of people become more important than lofty judgments. One should have an attitude that seeks to lift people up instead of dragging them down. No one ever loses by showing honor and kindness to others or by doing good unto them.

A person who is full of pride and selfish ambition and refuses to humble himself before God and others is guaranteed a big tumble. Proverbs 29:23 says, "A man's pride shall bring him low: but honour shall uphold the humble in spirit." He cannot walk with his nose in the air, ignoring all, and keep his direction. It is essential that a person walk with awareness of those that are on either side of him, or that stand in the pathway before him in need of help. If one is to have honor, he must not only be considerate of his own needs, but of those of others.

True kindness begins with humility. What is humility? Humility is absence of pride and absence of wrath. It is putting self in the proper perspective, not thinking more highly of oneself than one should. It is not self-depreciating or self-glory. Someone once said to think of self as neither worm nor wonder. Humility is recognizing you are not enough, but that you need God.

An unknown author wrote,

> Humility is perpetual quietness of heart. It is never to be fretted or vexed, irritable or sore. To wonder at nothing that is done to me, to feel nothing done against me. It is to be at rest when nobody praises me, and when I am blamed or despised, it is to have a blessed home in myself where I can go in and shut the door, and kneel to my Father in secret and be at peace, as in a deep sea of calmness when all around and about is trouble. [2]

After his discoveries in science, Sir Isaac Newton felt the humbleness of man and stated it like this:

> I do not know what I may appear to the world; but to myself I seem only like a boy playing upon the seashore, and diverting myself by now and then finding a pebble, or a

> prettier shell more than ordinary, while the great ocean of truth lies all undiscovered before me. [3]

Humility is a needy spirit that is sufficient only in God and not in self. When the church of Laodicea felt like they did not need anything and said, "I am rich, and increased with goods, and have need of nothing" (Revelation 3:17), that is when the Lord said they were poor, miserable, blind, wretched and naked. It is not how you see yourself only, but how God sees you. Humility is putting God on the throne of the heart and then kneeling before Him in worship and submission to His Word in dealing with others. It is exalting God to His rightful place and acknowledging Him in all things.

Franz Joseph Haydn, the famous composer, gave a great example of this in 1808, just a year before his death. A grand performance of his outstanding oratorio *The Creation* took place in Vienna. The composer himself was there for the occasion. Old and feeble, he was brought into the great hall in a wheelchair. His presence caused an electrifying enthusiasm in the audience.

As the orchestra and chorus burst forth with full power into the passage, "And there was light," a crescendo of applause broke out.

Moved by this response, the elderly musician struggled to his feet. Summoning all his strength, he raised his trembling arms upward, crying, "NO! NO! Not from me, but from thence—from Heaven above comes all!" Although he fell back exhausted in his chair and had to be carried from the hall, the old master had made his point in a dramatic and unforgettable manner. [4]

Humility is not being puffed up, angry or resentful. It reaches up for divine help. It does not strive, become bitter or resentful, accuse, justify or point fingers, but realizes the weakness within and asks for God's strength in the hour of temptation. God will never let anyone down who calls upon Him, for He honors the humble. The Apostle James said it this way: "But he giveth more grace. Wherefore he saith, God resisteth the proud, but giveth grace unto the humble" (James 4:6).

Unassuming humility is the way to riches and honor because the humble in heart is always concerned about the other person; self does not dominate. "By humility and the fear of the Lord are riches, and honour, and life" (Proverbs 22:4). There it is in a nutshell! True life, riches and honour are not attained through pushy, selfish or arrogant know-it-all attitudes, but through a kind, caring spirit and an awe and awareness of who God is. Solomon said it well: "Before destruction the heart of man is haughty, and before honour is humility" (Proverbs 18:12). Man chooses his destiny by his attitude toward God and others!

Elisha, the son of Shaphat, was doing his daily job plowing with twelve yoke of oxen when Elijah the prophet passed by and cast his mantle upon him. Elisha felt a call in that simple gesture and left all to follow Elijah. He did not start off being Elijah's partner, but he began as his servant. I Kings 19:21 says, "Then he arose, and went after Elijah, and ministered unto him." When Elijah was translated into the heavens some time later, Elisha received the thing he desired: Elijah's mantle. As it floated down from the chariot of fire, Elisha picked it up and smote the waters of the river of Jordan, saying, "Where is the Lord God of Elijah?" (II Kings 2:14). Immediately the waters parted and he walked across on dry land.

Later in his journey he came to the city of Shunem, where he was perceived as a man of God. He went from a humble, caring servant who ministered to the great Elijah, to a respected man of God himself. His attitude determined his destination. Because Elisha was willing to minister in kindness to Elijah and show honor to him, God returned his kindness by giving him his heart's desire.

Seven:

Kindness is Honoring One Another

HONOR ONE ANOTHER

On May 12, 1864, the 36th Regiment Massachusetts Volunteers became a part of one of the longest and deadliest battles of the Civil War. When they were called to battle, their destination was a point near Spotslvania Court House, where General Robert E. Lee's troops had established a powerful position. One of Lee's aims was to stop the forces of General Ulysses S. Grant from getting closer to the capital, Richmond, only 50 miles to the south.

On that early May morning, Sergeant Jerome Pierce and his regiment descended into a swampy thicket and then slogged through mud and rain toward a rolling meadow. As the men marched forward, the din of the battle resounded on every side. "Clubbed muskets and bayonets were used freely, as the rain poured down in sheets and the trenches ran red with blood," historian Joseph P. Cullen wrote. "The wounded and dying of both sides were trampled into the mud to drown or suffocate."

"By early afternoon," according to historian Ed Raus, "the deafening roar of battle could not drown out the hellish shrieks and screams of the wounded. The bullets seemed to fill the air as thick as raindrops." At some point during this bloody battle, a bullet ripped through the heart of Sergeant Pierce. Later his body was shoveled into a hastily dug grave that was crudely marked.

Several years after the Battle of the Bloody Angle, Andrew Birdsall, superintendent of the National Cemetery at Fredericksburg and a Union veteran, received a letter with $100.00 in it from a Massachusetts family he did not know. They asked him to try and locate the grave of Jerome Pierce and re-enter his remains at the Fredericksburg National Cemetery.

Superintendent Birdsall located Jerome's grave and moved it to Maryre's Heights, a Confederate stronghold converted into the National Cemetery. The final resting place for Jerome was marked by a small stub of a stone. Lucy, his wife, had asked that he be remembered with flowers from time to time, and for over 130 years this soldier has been remembered by strangers in a land where he had been the enemy. Recently one of Mr. Birdsall's daughters, Alive Abernathy, said, "We must never forget Jerome."

> And [each May] more than 130 years after Sergeant Pierce fell dead, his grave [is] honored as usual with the same spirit of respect and reconciliation that has healed the country. He has no direct descendants to honor him as he lied on this peaceful hillside—the home for so many of the brave. Instead, Jerome Pierce left something else; because of his sacrifice, and the sacrifice of so many others, countless millions the world over live today in freedom. [1]

What a beautiful gesture of honor to an unknown man simply because of the request of a hurting family. May the world seek to honor one another not only in death, but in living. Paul the Apostle wrote, "Be kindly affectioned one to another with brotherly love; in *honour* preferring one another" (Romans 12:10).

"Likewise, ye younger, submit yourselves unto the elder. Yea, *all of you* be subject one to another, and be clothed with humility: for God resisteth the proud, and giveth grace to the humble" (I Peter 5:5).

Again the Word whispers to our heart in challenging tones about subjects we would like to shut out: honoring others, humility, preference for another, submission one to another. How can anyone dishonor man and honor God at the same time? It is impossible! The two will not mix.

The Apostle James wrote about it. He said,

> Therewith bless we God, even the Father; and therewith curse we men, which are made after the similitude of God. Out of the same mouth proceedeth blessing and cursing. My brethren these things ought not so to be. Doth a fountain send forth at the same place sweet water and bitter? Can the fig tree, my brethren, bear olive berries? either a vine, figs? so can no fountain both yield salt water and fresh (James 3:9,12).

It is necessary to honor or bless one another. The blessing that is given to someone else will have a boomerang effect.

The scripture says it over and over, "Give and it shall be given unto you." It is an age-old truth. If you want to be blessed, you must bless others. If you want kindness shown to you, you must be kind. It is time to take note of others' good points and quit pointing an accusing finger, seeing only the bad.

Dr. Bellows wrote these noteworthy words to consider. "When a man does a noble act, date him from that. Forget his faults. Let his noble act be the standpoint from which you regard him."[2]

Talking about your neighbor's faults, failures and shortcomings is ugly, unprofitable and very displeasing to God. If you know of evil in others, seek to learn to mention it only to God. Pray for them, for prayer is a wonderful thing in correcting evil. The Apostle Peter wrote, "Honour all men. Love the brotherhood. Fear God. Honour the king" (I Peter 2:17).

He said *all men*. This includes bellhops, taxi drivers, waitresses, janitors, secretaries—the list is endless. It means having a kind word for everyone you meet and showing respect to them regardless of their position. A great person is one who treats everyone great, not just those with titles.

Honor is showing confidence in those who have more experience or knowledge than you do. Such was the case of Ruth, whose story is told in the Old Testament. Naomi, Ruth's mother-in-law, made an impression on her that penetrated deep within her soul. When the day came for Naomi to return to her homeland, Ruth spoke the beautiful words,

> Intreat me not to leave thee, or to return from following after thee: for whither thou goest, I will go; and where thou lodgest, I will lodge: thy people shall be my people, and thy God my God. Where thou diest, will I die, and there will I be buried: the Lord do so to me, and more also, if ought but death part thee and me (Ruth 1:16-17).

She was really saying, "Naomi, I respect and honor you. You have made an impact on my life, and I do not want to be severed from that influence. I love you so much that I want to stay with you and learn more of you and your God."

She also honored Naomi by following her advice and being kind to her after they reached Bethlehem. The scripture says that Ruth was a kind woman. Boaz, Naomi's kinsman, said to her, "Blessed be thou of the Lord, my daughter: for thou hast shewed more kindness in the latter end than at the beginning...for all the city of my people doth know that thou art a virtuous woman" (Ruth 3:10-11).

To honor one another is to seek the good for each other. It is to put pettiness aside and rejoice with each other if the occasion calls for it. It is to build a person's confidence and help him to walk tall while facing life's difficulties. Honor should not be hoarded, but dished out liberally to as many as deserve it. Look for ways to honor people and you will become much happier and fulfilled, for you cannot fill the purse of another without becoming richer yourself.

HONOR YOUR FATHER AND MOTHER

From the pages of old, down through the centuries, amid the babble of human reasoning, there remains this truth: "Honor thy father and thy mother; that thy days may be long upon the land which the Lord thy God giveth thee" (Exodus 20:12). It was the first commandment with promise. God first gave it to Moses on Mt. Sinai. Then when a new generation came on the scene he reiterated it in their hearing. "Honour thy father and thy mother, as the Lord thy God hath commanded thee" (Deuteronomy 5:16). It is referred to throughout the scriptures. Again in the New Testament, Jesus told the rich young ruler to keep the commandments and listed this as one (Matthew 19:19).

War is on! With the onslaught of disrespect aimed towards the family in the entertainment world, gradually the honor and respect is crumbling away. Questioning replaces trust, stubbornness replaces submission, selfishness becomes a way of life instead of selflessness. Division, restlessness and doing your own thing—instead of working together—becomes the norm.

The deplorable state of many families would lead one to believe that there is no hope and that family life is beyond repair. This is not true! Where there is God, there is hope. God is not dead! Only man's love for Him, His Word and each other, have died. God is not the problem—the lack of God is the problem. What can a society expect that chooses to take away the reverence for the Bible? The world is blatantly choosing man's way over God's way, and man's way always fails. Man's way and wisdom are not enough, as much as he would desire them to be. Families cannot have true love and be successful in their relationships without God being a part of them.

What would the Founding Fathers think if they knew that children in some of America's public schools today would be taking guns to school to kill one another, or a small number of children would be murdering their own parents without remorse? Where did the breakdown begin? How could a nation that was God-fearing and founded on the Bible have drifted so far in just 200 years or more? What went wrong? Why was the Bible taken out of schools and placed in the prisons instead?

The Bible, which breeds honor and respect, has been done away with in many cases, and replaced by violence, selfishness and greed. You cannot have an honor system without God. It is impossible to treat one another right without first respecting God.

When did people become so sophisticated that they think they have more brains than God, and do not need His Word? George Washington, our first president, knew otherwise. He said, "It is impossible to rightly govern the world without God and the Bible."

If the core of America is going to be saved from the rottenness that is now causing such decay among her children, she has got to come back to that which made America great in the beginning. President Woodrow Wilson said, "I ask every man and woman in this audience, that from this day on they will realize that part of the destiny of America lies in their daily perusal of this great Book."

The truth is that for people to be able to honor their father and mother properly, it is essential for there to be a foundation of biblical principles instilled within the heart. Your neighbor may choose not to read the Bible, the government may rudely deny the Bible's right to be in your child's classroom, but you as an individual can choose to read it yourself, and instill it in your children or those over whom you have influence.

HONOR THE AGED

Gertrude Cockerell wrote a tract entitled, *The Last Decade*, in 1914. She said,

> In all walks of life are to be found the aged, who for positive achievement, or as conquerors over disability and circumstances, wear ever on their brows the laurel leaves of conquest. They are still men and women of affairs, they have not dropped out of the arena of active life, or, if so, yet wield influence that tells upon life, whether spiritual, moral, or mental. Here and there one thus stands out—a weather-beaten rock, that has withstood the storms and ravages of time.

These conquerors need to be honored. This commandment is given in Leviticus 19:32: "Thou shalt rise up before the hoary head, and honour the face of the old man, and fear thy God: I am the Lord." *Hoary* is white or gray with age. In the New Testament the aged widows were considered so important that the Apostles took time to appoint seven deacons to help care for their needs. They are to be honored as well as looked after. They are not to be put on a shelf and forgotten about; they are not to be simply tolerated. They are to be esteemed and highly respected.

We are commanded not to rebuke an elder, but to intreat him as a father, to treat the elder women as mothers, and to honour widows (I Timothy 5:1-3). They are to be well cared for and treated as beloved and special. No one gets too old that he does not need a friend or someone to listen to him. Everyone needs recognition as being important, not treated as someone taking up space.

Blessings are bestowed upon the person who shows honor and kindness. This is proven in many ways. One such account was a story that was told by a man who married into a family with an wealthy aged aunt who was tolerated, but not cherished or respected. He and his wife went to this aunt's home where many members of the family had gathered together. All the younger ones went off by themselves, so he began talking with the aunt. As he showed interest in the history of the house, she began to show him around, pointing out treasures of her past. Each one had a story and he listened intently while she talked as they passed from room to room. Finally they came to the garage. When she opened the door, he caught sight of a valuable antique Packard. She told him of the days when she and her husband used to drive in it and as she lived those bygone days her face lit up. Then she turned to the young man and with tears in her eyes told him she wanted him to have the car.

He immediately told her that he could not accept the car because he was not related to her except through marriage, and other members of the family would want it. She assured him that she knew they wanted it, but because they did not have time for her, she did not want to give it to them. He received because he gave her what she was lacking most: honor, kindness, respect and a listening ear. Her riches were empty, her idle moments haunting, but when she met someone that honored her with kind attention and care, she wanted to give something back to him.

Some years ago *Guideposts* magazine printed a story about a young woman who wanted to see and feel what the elderly saw and felt because of their age. She dressed up like a older person and used wigs, makeup and clothing to play the role. She was appalled at the treatment she received. Younger children teased her and threw rocks at her, she was ignored in stores, and was often looked down upon by many simply because she tottered instead of walking with a spring in her step. She was treated with disgust when she pretended to be hard of hearing. She lived out several months in this disguise and said she was never treated so badly in all her life.

It is a sad day when the elderly are treated with neglect, shoved aside for the more youthful beauties and banished to the less-than-best part of the house simply because they are old. The aged are to be honored and treated with kindness. By observing how the adults treat the aged, the children learn how to show proper respect, kindness and honor: the most neglected elements by some people in today's modern society.

Richard DeHaan tells how an elderly couple from Montana visited him in his office. Their presence emphasized the "generation gap." Their steps were faltering, their eyesight failing, and their hearing diminishing. He said he usually moves at a brisk pace, but as he slowed down to walk beside them it seemed as if he were almost standing still. He had to repeat his words over and over again to accommodate their deafness.

While he was with them he prayed silently, "O Lord, help me always to be patient and understanding with all who are aged, not in a condescending way, not out of pity, but because of a genuine respect for those who have walked life's pathway before me, endured its trials, and waged its battles."

He went on to challenge this generation with these words:

> May all of us who still enjoy the vigor of good health and do not yet feel the frailties of the declining years, treat those elderly saints with proper esteem. Also let us do everything we possibly can to bridge the gap and gladden the hearts of those who have earned their place in God's *gallery of honor!* [3]

Billy Graham said, "The neglect of older people is becoming an increasing sin in America." [4]

It is time to show honor to the aged more than ever before in the face of the crumbling of time-honored values. Youth has its beauty but age has a beauty all its own. Old lace is more valuable than new lace, just as old trees are more beautiful than new trees. There is beauty in the older generation: a beauty of style, dignity and graciousness. Their experience is worth more than many books. It is time to listen to them and to let them know they are appreciated and loved.

Someone asked, "Is there anything more beautiful in life than a boy and girl clasping clean hands and pure hearts in the path of marriage?" And the answer is given, "Yes, there is a more beautiful thing; it is the spectacle of an old man and an old woman finishing their journey together on that path. Their hands are gnarled but still clasped; their faces are seamed but still radiant; their hearts are tired and bowed down but still strong. They have proved the happiness of marriage and have vindicated it from the jeers of cynics." [5]

In the following poem, Ella Wheeler Wilcox paints a picture of growing older:

The days grow shorter, the nights grow longer;
The tear comes quicker, the laugh comes slower.
But all true things in the world seem truer,
And the better things of earth seem best,
And friends are dearer, as friends are fewer,
And love is all as our sun dips west.
Then let us clasp hands as we walk together,
And let us speak softly in low, sweet tones,
For no man knows on the morrow whether
We two pass on—or but one alone. [6]

Life is not over just because someone passes the age of 65; for many it is the most blessed time of life. Someone said,

> Life really begins at eighty. Moses was eighty years of age when God called him to the leadership of Israel. Cato, at eighty, began the study of Greek; Tennyson, at eighty, wrote, "Crossing the Bar;" George Bernard Shaw has written some of his most famous plays while in his eight-

> ies; Scott, the commentator, began the study of Hebrew at eighty-seven; Verdi wrote "Ave Maria" at eighty-five; many judges of the Supreme Court have been nearer eighty than seventy; Goethe wrote Faust when past eighty; Simonides won a prize for poetry when past eighty; Dr. Howard A. Kelly continued to be a world-famous cancer specialist when past eighty. [7]

Growing older may have its moments of regrets and disappointments, but it also has its hours of truth and gladness. The years lived by older people are filled with valuable experience and wisdom. They should be respected and treated with kindness.

This is the day to love and show kindness, honor and respect to the older people, for as their strength diminishes, their need for love remains the same. No one ever outgrows love, and there is never anyone who gets too old who does not need respect and kindness. The emotional structures of men and women make it necessary for them to have respect and honor in order to grow and become. People who are treated like a mangy dog many times shrivel and die within. The light goes out of the eyes and the glow for living fades. It is essential to respect the older generation, for they are the true gold of the land.

HUSBANDS AND WIVES HONOR ONE ANOTHER

In the Talmud there is a story of a peasant worker who fell in love with the daughter of his wealthy employer. She returned his love and, despite her father's violent objections, married him. Aware of her husband's ardent love for learning, she insisted that he go to the great rabbinical academy at Jerusalem to quench his intellectual thirst. He studied for twelve years while she, disowned by her family, suffered in poverty and loneliness. Though still eager for advanced studies, he returned home. When he reached the door of his house, he overheard his wife saying to a neighbor that even though the pain of separation seemed more than she could bear, she hoped and prayed that he would return to the academy for further study.

Without a word to anyone, he went back to the school for twelve years more of study. Once again he turned determined footsteps toward his native village, but this time all Palestine was singing his praises as the most brilliant and scholarly mind of his generation. As he entered the market place, he was caught in the crowd of a reception committee that had gathered to honor their native son. While people were pressing about him, he saw a woman—her body bent, her face wrinkled—desperately trying to break through to reach him.

Suddenly he realized that this prematurely old woman, whom the milling crowd ignored and pushed back, was his beloved wife.

"Let her through," he shouted. "Let her through. It is she, not I, whom you should honor—she who sacrificed while I studied. Had it not been for her willingness to work and wait, to serve and suffer, I would be today a peasant laborer and not Rabbi Akeba." [8]

The man was a true hero, giving honor to whom honor was due. There is a powerful scripture often overlooked that needs to be examined more. Peter dealt with the husband-and-wife relationship. In I Peter 3:1 he told the wives to be in subjection to their own husbands. Then in verse 7 he had a word for the husbands. "Likewise, ye husbands, dwell with them according to knowledge, giving *honour* unto the wife, as unto the weaker vessel, and as being *heirs together* of the grace of life; that your prayers be not hindered."

The way a man treats his wife determines whether he will get his prayers answered or not. The wife is not a piece of property to be dominated by brute force. She is to be honored as a partner, and together they are to share one another's dreams and plans.

It does matter to God how a husband and wife care for one another. It is not pleasing to Him when married couples try to lift holy hands to Him and then hit each other, or scream uncomplimentary words at one another. Husbands and wives should be courteous to one another. Although some Hollywood producers have made a joke of the marital relationship by showing examples of chaos, rudeness and infidelity, it is no joke to God.

Courtesy, kindness and respect are the foundations upon which a good marriage is built. Carol Haynes expresses it well in the following poem.

Any Wife or Husband

Let us be guests in one another's house
With deferential "No" and courteous "Yes;"
Let us avoid all sullen silences;
We should find fresh and sprightly things to say;

Let us knock gently at each other's heart,
Glad of a chance to look within—and yet
Let us remember that to force one's way
Is the unpardoned breach of etiquette.

So shall I be hostess—you, the host—
Until all need for entertainment ends;

We shall be lovers when the last door shuts,
But what is better still—we shall be friends. [9]

To be a friend is to understand one another and each other's place in the home. God made man the leader, not the dictator. To lead means to direct, guide or shepherd. As head over a church, a pastor does not beat up his people, but guides them in the right way. What executive of a large company would abuse those under his authority? None that was successful. He would encourage, cheer them on, and help them to become better employees. It is the same with a husband. He should want his wife to feel fulfilled, cherished and loved. She is not a second-rate citizen just because she is told to submit. There is a chain of authority and God instituted it because anything with two heads is a freak. The two must work together, honoring each other's position, not demeaning it. It is not wondering who is the most important; both are important, but with different job assignments. Honor, respect and kindness must be a part of the marriage relationship in order for prayers to not be hindered and for there to be true friendship.

If a marriage is stormy, tempestuous and founded upon snarling words, it is because a carnal spirit has not submitted to God. If one does not submit first to God, it is impossible to properly submit to one another.

The Apostle James said it well:

> From whence come wars and fightings among you? come they not hence, even of your lusts that war in your members? Ye lust, and have not: ye kill, and desire to have, and cannot obtain: ye fight and war, yet ye have not, because ye ask not. Ye ask, and receive not, because ye ask amiss, that ye may consume it upon your lusts. Submit yourselves therefore to God. Resist the devil, and he will flee from you. Draw nigh to God, and he will draw nigh to you. Humble yourselves in the sight of the Lord, and he shall lift you up (James 4:1-3,7,10).

Now is the time for husbands and wives to be kind and start honoring one another in deed and in speech. It is time to remember important dates and the special likes or dislikes of one another. It is time to build up the home.

Amid all the cares of married life, in spite of the toils, take time to value each other. When days are dark and troubles come, stick together, facing the storm as one. Do not become angry at one another because of what is happening around you. Never let your hearts grow cold, but take the time to be friends and listen to each other's dreams, thoughts and considerations.

Love does not embarrass one another, but edifies. It seeks to speak of the good and not proclaim the bad. Love protects and cares about the feelings of the other one. Love will always find a way to spare another's feelings.

One wife who cared more about her husband than she did herself manifested it in an unique way. Andrew Meredith shares the story.

> There was once a young bride in a small English village who had just been married. At the conclusion of the ceremony the bridegroom, a bit reluctant and hesitant, signed the parish register with an X mark. His charming young bride followed him, and likewise made her "X."
>
> "Why, Mary," whispered the minister's wife, "you can write your name. You were one of the best scholars in the parish school."
>
> "Yes," the young woman replied, "but John cannot write, and I would not shame him for the world. I will teach him to write, and then I can join with him in the pleasure of writing our names." [10]

Eight:

Kindness is Rewarded

Walter B. Knight tells the story of the wealthy nobleman in Italy who had grown tired of life. He had everything one could wish for except happiness. He said, "I am weary of life. I will go to the river and end my life."

As he walked along, he felt a little hand tugging at his trousers. Looking down, he saw a frail, hungry-looking little boy who pleaded, "There are six of us. We are dying for want of food!"

The nobleman thought, "Why should I not relieve this wretched family? I have the money." Following the little boy, he entered a scene of misery, sickness and want. He opened his purse and he emptied all of its contents, saying, "I'll return tomorrow, and I will share with you more of the good things which God has given to me in abundance!"

He left that scene of want and wretchedness, rejoicing, with no thought of ending his life. This is the reward of kindness. It gives a glow like nothing else.

"If you want to be miserable, think much about yourself, about what you want, what you like, what respect people ought to pay you, and what people think of you" (Charles Kingsley). "It is when we forget ourselves that we do things that are remembered" (Eugene P. Bertin).

Many years ago a lonely traveler stopped one Sunday morning for the worship service at a little country church in Georgia. After the service he was warmly greeted by the people, but was never seen there again.

Quiet a few years later in Washington, New Jersey, Robert B. Brown, age ninety, died. Mr. Brown bequeathed his entire estate to the little country church that had befriended him when he was just a lonely traveler. At the time of Mr. Brown's death, his stocks were worth $178,302.50.

The deceased's attorney, Martin B. Bry-Nildsen, in informing the church of the bequest, wrote: "My client told me that on a Sunday morning years ago, when he was traveling through Georgia, he felt sad and lonely. He stopped at your church and was met with a very friendly welcome. He never forgot the kindness you showed him. He did not have any church affiliation and said, 'I want to give what I have to that little church.'"

The church members were very surprised when they received the money from Mr. Brown's attorney. No one could recall Mr. Brown's visit to the church. They were always kind to everyone and Mr. Brown had been the recipient of their usual kindness and courtesy.

Walter B. Knight wrote,

> Life is a boomerang.
> What we are and do comes back to us.
> Each one is the inheritor of himself.
> For life is the mirror of king and slave,
> 'Tis just what we are and do;
> Then give to the world the best you have,
> And the best will come back to you! [1]

Ecclesiastes 11:1 says, "Cast thy bread upon the waters: for thou shalt find it after many days."

Horace Mann defined the reward of kindness in the following discourse:

> Doing nothing for others is the undoing of one's self. We must be purposely kind and generous or we miss the best part of existence. The heart that goes out of itself gets large and full of joy. This is the great secret of the inner life. We do ourselves the most good doing something for others. [2]

A person's kindness should not always be limited to those who are his friends. Jesus said to love your enemies, and do good to them that despitefully use you. In so doing your reward would be great.

> And ye shall be the children of the Highest; for he is kind unto the unthankful and to the evil. Be ye therefore merciful, as your Father also is merciful. Judge not, and ye shall not be judged: condemn not, and ye shall not be condemned: forgive, and ye shall be forgiven; Give, and it shall be given unto you; good measure, pressed down, and shaken together, and running over, shall men give into your bosom, For with the same measure that ye mete withal it shall be measured to you again (Luke 6:35-38).

As far as an individual is concerned, it does not matter so much if other people are unkind, but it does matter how a person reacts to an offense, for in time, both the offenders and the receivers will receive the same treatment (good or bad) back unto themselves.

God will give to every person his just reward. Everyone will receive something, so it might as well be something good.

> [God] will render to every man according to his deeds: to them who by patient continuance in well doing seek for glory and honour and immortality, eternal life: but unto them that are contentious, and do not obey the truth, but obey unrighteousness, indignation and wrath, tribulation and anguish, upon every soul of man that doeth evil, of the Jew first, and also of the Gentile; but glory, honour, and peace, to every man that worketh good (Romans 2:6-10).

Notice the first thing which brings tribulation and anguish is contention and the last thing is wrath. Both are the opposite of honor, kindness and humility. Honor and kindness seek to bring unity and consideration, whereas humility is absence of wrathful indignation.

Contention is to be avoided like the plague. It brings only disaster and disease of the soul. It is a quarrelsome attitude which manifests itself in an act of strife, a spirit of discord which keeps things stirred up. It is a point maintained in an argument in a know-it-all, belligerent attitude. It cares not for the people involved; it cares only to be right.

In Brussels, Belgium, a house burned to the ground while two fire brigades lost time arguing about who was to put out the blaze. The volunteer fire company in Denderleeuw was first on the scene. The full-time fire brigade from nearby Aalst soon joined them. When the Denderleeuw fire chief said his company had priority on the job, the Aalst firemen rolled up their hoses. But the fire got out of hand, so the Denderleeuw firemen called back the Aalst brigade and eventually had to summon a third company from Liedekerke. The house was destroyed, and two neighboring houses were damaged. *They were more concerned with who was right* than they were with saving the house from burning down. No one received any honor out of this episode, only shame and distress.

Daily while a major crisis abounds around us which results in people being hurt deeply, there are those with contentious spirits that are involved in the crisis who care more about proving they are right than about the person who is being hurt. Does being right coupled with a bad attitude influence anyone towards Christ or rightness? Is the spiritual house burning down? Is the world headed towards destructive fire while the church outshouts one another in heated, quarreling debates?

Does the church have glory, honor and peace or anguish and tribulation?

If being contentious brings anguish, what brings peace and honor? He that does good works. Paul wrote in Titus 2:7, "In all things shewing thyself a pattern of good works...." *All things* means everything, including relationships between each other. It is needful to develop a lifestyle which includes a pattern of good works, for he that works good will receive glory, honor and peace.

It is not enough to be considered rich in this world's goods or successful by the world's standards. This does not bring honor or peace. Consider the following story. John D. Rockefeller, Sr. became a millionaire at age 33. At age 43, he controlled the biggest company in the world. At age 53, he was the richest man on earth and the world's only billionaire.

Then he developed a sickness called alopecia, where the hair of his head dropped off, his eyelashes and eyebrows disappeared, and he was shrunken like a mummy. His weekly income was one million dollars, but he was able to digest milk and crackers only. He was so hated in Pennsylvania that he had to have bodyguards day and night. He could not sleep, stopped smiling and enjoyed nothing.

When the doctors predicted he would not live over one year, he got to thinking during his sleepless nights about his millions. He realized that he could not take one dime into the next world. So he started helping churches, the poor and needy. He established the Rockefeller Foundation whose funding of medical research led to the discovery of penicillin and other wonder drugs. At the age of 54, Mr. Rockefeller began to sleep well, eat and enjoy life and lived to be 98 years old. *He received honor and peace because he started doing good instead of thinking only of himself.*

A person who thinks only of his own self is miserable. I well remember an incident during the 1993 Christmas holidays which proves this.

While shopping in Macy's department store, I stepped up to the counter to be waited on. Facing me on the other side was a lady already being waited on by another clerk. Suddenly an elderly lady wandered in from outside and said in a voice that could be heard by all standing there, "I need you to help me with my bill I received in the mail. I came here once before, but found that the office upstairs had been closed."

Then the clerk paused long enough to respond to her statement, telling her it was true, the office had been closed. She told her she would have to call the main office. The elderly woman seemed not to have heard her, and again said, "I need to talk to you about my bill."

The clerk kindly took the time and told her that she would be glad to help her as soon as she finished with the lady with whom she was transacting business. So the older woman shuffled over to the side and began waiting her turn.

The thing that amazed me was the reaction of the young woman whom the clerk was helping. She said in loud tones so all could hear, "It is just not right. Why can't people wait their turn in line? I know she is elderly, but she should learn to wait like everyone else." She continued and said, "I am very upset because of this. That woman caused me to have to wait while you [the clerk] took time to answer her questions, and my baby is screaming. It's just not right." She continued to steam, "Why can't these people wait their turn like everybody else?"

Then after she had spouted off, she just kept shaking her head back and forth muttering to herself about the injustice of someone taking up her time and not waiting her turn.

First of all, the baby was not screaming at all. He was making soft gurgling sounds while sitting in his stroller. Secondly, I was appalled at the young woman's selfishness, and thought, "Is this the kind of young adult this generation is producing?" God forbid! I could not help but remember that when I was a child, if Grandma came into the room and I was sitting down, Grandma got my chair. If an elderly person became a little confused and busted in on the conversation, we were taught to respect the elders, even if it inconvenienced us.

Here I was witnessing a scene that repulsed me. The whole scenario took about 1½ minutes. The young woman was steaming over less than two minutes of waiting and showed great disrespect toward her elders. It clearly spoke to all standing there: she was self-centered to a sickening degree. I mulled it over and over and came up with this conclusion: Selfishness has become like a canker in our society. People often think only of themselves and do not even realize it.

I thought of Florence Nightingale who gave up a life of selfishness and the butterfly existence of a society deb to care for the sick, the wounded, the young and the elderly. She was not spouting to those around her about someone infringing on her time; she served selflessly, considering the needs of others around her.

The young woman standing at the counter at Macy's did not receive honor that day. The clerk, as well as others standing around, were clearly stunned by the heated outburst from this well-dressed, immaculately groomed woman who had not learned the secret to happiness. She was a miserable woman because of her attitude towards others.

Abraham Lincoln said what this generation needs to be reminded of: "To ease another's heartache is to forget one's own." One of the reasons why our nation is surrounded by such violence and pain is because we have become a nation that in many respects cares only for "our four and no more," and sometimes not even that. It is time to start showing a real interest in our fellow man. True heartfelt kindness is greatly needed in these days of sickening violence.

The Apostle Paul, moved by the inspiration of the Holy Ghost, penned the words, "Glory, honor and peace to every man that worketh good" (Romans 2:10). He said, "In all things shewing thyself a pattern of good works" (Titus 2:7). This woman was developing a pattern of works and attitudes, but they were not good. Just as a worm gets inside a juicy, red, polished apple, she had allowed a cankerworm of selfishness to crawl inside of her. It was destroying the potential of good works that the Lord was so desirous for her to have.

Suppose that, instead of this selfish woman, the person who was being waited on by the clerk was the Lord Jesus Christ. What would He have done? How would He have acted? My mind goes to the incident when the disciples were gathered in a room at Simon's house, eating and enjoying the privilege of being first in line. They were interrupted by a woman who came in and poured spikenard on the feet of Jesus, wiping them with her hair.

The disciples did not like it and wanted to rebuke her, but Jesus took up for her. He honored her and showed kindness and respect to her. He could have said along with the disciples, "What right does this woman have coming in here? First of all, she does not belong here, and secondly, she is wasting a precious commodity that could be used for the poor."

True, the elderly woman that wandered into the store was not doing a special deed that ministered to the Lord Jesus, but Christ would have treated her with respect just as He did the woman who washed His feet. Society was not kind to her, neither did they show her respect. They looked down upon her, but Jesus gave her respect. He showed her honor by treating her with kindness, although she did not deserve it.

The important thing to remember is, Christians are the representatives of Christ on earth. How they treat others is *supposedly* out of the spirit of Christ that they represent to those around them. Selfishness demands its rights and there are a lot of perpetuators of this new philosophy. It is a philosophy that is not found in the Word of God, but is hatched out of the fumes of death and hell. It acts as a vise that slowly squeezes the life from anyone who participates in its doctrines.

Patterns for life should be purchased from the tried and true Word of God, and not from the new company that is polished but empty, full of high-sounding phrases. The Book says *showing yourself a pattern of good works*. What are you showing the world, selfishness or selflessness?

Remember, the word "good" has "GOD" in it, and you cannot be good without the influence of God. So keep close to God and His Word and you will start developing a storehouse of patterns of good works.

An account by J.R. Miller shows how one man's effort to do this stopped a war for one hour.

> It was at Fredericksburg, after a bloody battle. Hundreds of Union soldiers lay wounded on the field. All night and all next day the space was swept by artillery from both armies, and no one could venture to the sufferers' relief. Agonizing cries for water were going up from where the wounded lay, but there was no response save the roar of the guns. One brave fellow behind the ramparts, a Southern soldier, felt that he could endure these piteous cries no longer. His compassion rose superior to his love of life.
>
> "General," said Richard Kirkland to his commander, "I can't stand this. Those poor souls out there have been praying for water all night, and all day, and it is more than I can bear. I ask permission to carry them water."

The general assured him that it would be instant death for him to appear upon the field, but he begged so earnestly that the officer, admiring his noble devotion to humanity, could not refuse his request. Provided with a supply of water, the brave soldier stepped over the wall and went on his Christ-like errand. From both sides wondering eyes looked on as he knelt by the nearest sufferer, and gently raising his head, held the cooling cup to his parched lips. At once the Union soldiers understood what the soldier in gray was doing for their own wounded comrades, and not a shot was fired. For an hour and a half he continued his work, giving drink to the thirsty, straightening cramped and mangled limbs, pillowing men's heads on their knapsacks, and spreading blankets and army coats over them, tenderly as a mother would cover her child; and all the while, until this angel-ministry was finished, the fusillade of death was hushed.

Again we must admire the heroism that led this brave soldier in gray so utterly to forget himself for the sake of doing a deed of mercy to his enemies. There is more grandeur in five minutes of self-renunciation than in a whole lifetime of self-interest and self-seeking. [3]

The honor shown to the hurting, thirsty and wounded was rewarded by a inner feeling that Richard Kirkland had done what he felt was right. He could now live with himself and look himself in the eye without regret or revulsion. If the wounded could have clapped that day, he would have enjoyed their applause as they sought to reward their hero and show their thanksgiving. Eternal rewards are in the hands of the Master for Him to give someday, but that day the act itself rewarded him.

Nine:

Kindness—Can It Be Brought Back?

On Sunday night, December 29, 1946, shortly after the first edition of the *Miami Herald* had gone to press, Timothy Sullivan answered the telephone on the city desk. "Please help me," a woman's voice pleaded. "My husband is bleeding to death."

Sullivan got the entire story. The man's name was Rudy Kovarik, from Dearborn, Michigan. They were on a vacation but he was sick and in the Biscayne Hospital. The AB RH-negative blood needed was not available at the hospital or through other sources. Without a transfusion, the doctors thought he might not live until morning.

What could the city editor do? A man was dying. A woman's heart was breaking. Then he got an idea. He called radio station WCBS, fourteen blocks away, where it was almost time for Walter Winchell to go on the air on a nationwide broadcast. The operator refused to let him talk to Winchell, but finally was persuaded to let him talk to Winchell's assistant. After giving the assistant information, he listened to see what the result would be.

Soon the telephones began to go wild at the *Herald* office, the police station, and the hospital. People from all over the nation were calling in to offer help, and people as far away as New York City began to board planes for Miami. Soon the corridors of the Biscayne Hospital were crowded.

The actual donor was a tourist from New York who heard the broadcast on his car radio, checked his Army dog tags for blood type, and drove two blocks to the hospital. In a few minutes his life-giving blood was flowing into the veins of the stricken man. A few weeks later, Rudy Kovarik walked up to the *Herald's* city desk to thank Timothy Sullivan for caring enough to do something about it.

When I read this story, my thoughts compared the 40's with the 90's. "Would this same story stir the hearts of the American people now, the way it did back then?" I thought. Is old-fashioned care and kindness on their way out? Honor, kindness and respect are still among us, but to what degree? To where did the care and the honor shown to one another in the 40's disappear? Is it possible that this generation can blindly go its own way without offering help and assistance to a fellow man who is in need?

Several years ago in Chicago, a girl was being stabbed 38 times and although people heard her cries for help, no one heeded them. Since that story appeared in the newspapers, there has been an increase in similar stories. It is difficult to comprehend the mentality of cruel and unfeeling people who simply do not care about someone in need, or those who do not regard the sanctity of human life.

A story entitled "Ticket to a Murder," written by Michael Bowker, appeared in the November 1996 issue of *Reader's Digest.* He tells of two women who were on duty at a convenience store in Eugene, Oregon, at 10:30 p.m. on Sunday, April 10, 1994. A half-hour before closing time, four rough-looking men entered the store, and one of the men yelled for one of the girls to open the cash register. Another man went towards the cooler to where the other girl was working. A few minutes later, he appeared with blood smeared across his shirt, pants and face.

One man began beating the girl at the cash register with a steel pipe over and over. While the blood splattered, another man yelled, "Can't you even kill a woman?" He then took out a knife and slashed her with it and stuck a pipe in her mouth.

There was a noise and the men thought it was some customers, so they fled. After they had left, the girl who had been beaten with the steel pipe ran to a house close by and the people there called the police.

When the police arrived, they found the other girl's dead body. Her skull had been brutally crushed. The bone-chilling climax to the whole story was when they admitted during questioning that they were Satanists whose goal that night was to kill somebody. Nineteen-year-old Michael James Hayward, who had done the actual killing, said, "If I had it to do over again, I wouldn't change anything. Her life, or any other person's life, means nothing to me."

James C. Hefley asked the question, "Where are the Samaritans?" He wrote,

> In New York City a mailman, shot by a sniper, is ordered from a building lobby because he is dripping blood.
>
> In Oklahoma City a woman gives birth unexpectedly—on a city sidewalk. Bystanders turn their faces. A taxi driver looks, then speeds away. A nearby hotel refuses a blanket.

In Dayton, Ohio, a dozen people see a woman drive her car into the Miami River. They watch indifferently as the woman climbs on the car's roof and screams that she can't swim. The woman drowns.

So many incidents like these have happened that the *Chicago Sun-Times* library now has a special file tabbed, *Apathy.* [1]

Not only have the respect and care for one another declined, but a terrible disease of name-calling has erupted in our society. As a boil shows a problem in the blood, likewise disrespect for another designates the putridness of the heart. "My old man," has replaced Dad or Father in many families. "Stupid," "Dumb," "Idiot," "Troublemaker" or "Ugly" have replaced names of children. "Pig" has replaced Police Officer. The list is endless.

Icy stares have replaced warm smiles in many places. "Every man for himself" has replaced old-fashioned kindness or courtesy in many circles. Drive-by shootings, gang-related murders, rapes and robberies are the norm in many of the larger cities. Where it used to be a person did not need to lock his door, now *one* lock is not enough.

In days gone by automobiles moved over to the right side of the road when there was a funeral procession. Men took their hats off in respect for the dead. Now they coldly try to cut in and pass by as quickly as possible. No one seems to have time to even respect the dead anymore. Although there are still those that show old-fashioned respect, not enough do. There is a plague of disrespect that has swept this country.

Where did old-fashioned kindness, respect and honor go? Who started the name-calling? How did a wife become an "old lady" or "witch?" Where did the breakdown begin? Why are there wedges between parents and children, husbands and wives, and members of society? Why isn't the minister respected like he used to be? When did a doctor become a "butcher" or a politician a "buzzard"? Has humility become a thing of the past? Is honoring your brother or sister outdated, replaced by pushing self forward? Where did honesty go? Have our own feelings become more important than the feelings of others? Can it be that self-gratification has become more important than meeting the needs of others?

The story is told of a strange dog who came to a preacher's house. The preacher's three sons became quite fond of it. It so happened that there were three white hairs in the animal's tail. One day an advertisement was seen in the newspaper about a lost dog which fitted that description perfectly. The minister and his three boys separated the three white hairs and removed them.

The real owner discovered where the straying dog had found a home and came to claim him. The dog showed every sign of recognition, so the man was ready to take him away. Quickly the minister spoke up, "Didn't you say the dog would be known by three white hairs in its tail?" The owner, unable to find the three hairs, was forced to leave.

The minister said later, "We kept the dog, but I lost my three boys for Christ." His sons no longer had confidence in what their father professed. He had not practiced what he preached.

Has this generation lost confidence in each other, the ministry, or its leadership? Has each of us been tempted to ride roughshod over that which is right in order to satisfy selfish whims, just as the father removed the three white hairs to keep the dog? What compromises have been made that have caused honor to be lost?

Honor is showing respect, consideration and courtesy to another. It is a sense of what is right, just and true, showing dignity and courage in the face of danger, and manifesting excellence of character, integrity, uprightness and purity that begets honor. It is consideration for the feelings of others. It is listening to their opinions with due respect even though they may be different from one's own.

Can honor, kindness and consideration for the feelings of others be restored in the home amongst family members, in the schools between teachers and students, in the government, churches and places of business? Is there hope for these things to be brought back? Can one person make a difference? Yes, but with a lot of work, prayer and endurance.

In seventeenth-century England, most public worship became a crime and thousands of churches were torn down. One man built a church, even then, that still stands. The reason for its endurance can be interpreted from the inscription found over the door:

> In the year 1653 when all things sacred throughout ye nation were either demolight or profane, Sir Robert Shirley, Baronet, founded this church whose singular praise it is to have done the best things in the worst times and hoped them in the most calamitous. [2]

People can give up and let honor go, or they can work at bringing it back into their family, church and government. Everything begins with the individual. Each person must work on himself first before starting on a neighbor. Being kind and showing honor to one another does not have to be a thing of the past. It can be an integral part of lives today, for it does not begin with outer forces; it begins within. That is where all changes first occur.

If kindness and honor are to be brought back, it is essential that each person start with his own world. The sad truth is that because of an overwhelming tide of dishonor and evil, many will stick their head in the sand like the proverbial ostrich and do nothing. Edmond Burke once made the remark, "All that is essential for the triumph of evil is that good men do nothing."[3]

The challenge for each one who desires for his children, friends and neighbors to live in a better world is to start doing something about it now. If you wait for things to get better, they never will; you have to make them change.

Can one person make a difference? During the American Revolution, anti-British sentiment was high in many of the colonies. A bill was presented to the Continental Congress which would have abolished English as the official American language in favor of German. The bill was defeated by one vote. One person can make a difference, for a nation is made up of many such persons. If we fail to care, then we disintegrate.

Dr. Laurence M. Gould, President Emeritus of Carleton College, said,

> I do not believe the greatest threat to our future is from bombs or guided missiles. I don't think our civilization will end that way. I think it will die when we no longer care. Arnold Toynbee has pointed out that nineteen of twenty-one civilizations have died from within and not by conquest from without. There were no bands playing and flags waving when these civilizations decayed. It happened slowly, in the quiet and in the dark when no one was aware.[4]

On the front cover of *Time* magazine's May 16, 1994 issue were these words: "There are no devils left in Hell—They are all in Rwanda." I turned to page three and read the following explanation of the cover: "In the bloodiest eruption of violence in years, hundreds of thousands have died or fled from the carnage in Central Africa. Is this the face of wars to come?"

Then I turned to page 57 and Nancy Gibbs shared the horror of it all. She talked about the rivers that normally swell with a rich red soil, but this year they are more swollen than ever. She wrote,

> First come the corpses of men and older boys, slain trying to protect their sisters and mothers. Then come the women

> and girls, flushed out from their hiding places and cut down. Last are the babies, who may bear no wounds; they are tossed alive into the water, to drown on their way downstream.

Soldiers of war used to respect and honor women and children; now in many cases, as in Rwanda, even that is gone. The cruelty and violence of a generation that is crazed by hatred has degenerated into vicious killing. Daniel Bellamy, who serves on the U.N. High Commission for Refugees and has encountered these killers at numerous roadblocks in the capital, wrote in the same article, "If you look in their eyes there is something there that is not in the eyes of normal people."

Several questions arise after one reads the account of this latest civil war in Rwanda. Number one: How can human beings degenerate into such callused, barbaric creatures? Number two: Are there unseen forces and spirits at work controlling these people, as intimated by Daniel Bellamy?

When the question arises about being controlled by spirits it is answered by the story that hooked the world in 1993 which I referred to in Chapter 5. The Associated Press reported that in Preston, England, two "cunning and wicked" eleven-year-old boys were convicted and imprisoned indefinitely for beating a toddler to death in a crime that stunned Britain and led to nationwide soul-searching.

The boys were ten when they lured two-year-old James Bulger from his mother at a Liverpool shopping mall. On February 12, 1993, they beat him with rocks and an iron bar along an isolated railroad track. Prosecutors said the boys dragged him 2½ miles to the tracks, partially stripped him, splattered him with blue paint and beat him. When his body was found, it had been sliced in half by a train. The judge said he suspected that violent films on video may in part be an explanation.

While Britain reels and rocks with an increase in juvenile violence, America's violence has also increased. There is so much happening now that it is difficult to keep up with it. There is danger in becoming inoculated with apathy and not really caring enough to do something about it. Serial rapist Kurt Newman assaulted and raped many women in Southern California, becoming more violent in his attacks. Finally in January 1993, he was convicted on fifty felony charges including rape, attempted murder, robbery and kidnapping. He is just one among many that makes up America's growing violent population. The strange thing about this case was when they arrested Kurt at his nice air-conditioned office, several found it hard to believe that this nice man could do anything so atrocious. He had never been arrested for anything before.

After the murder of Nicole Simpson, the July 4, 1994 issue of *Time* had on its cover, "When Violence Hits Home." The increase in domestic abuse in America is shocking and appalling. Jill Smalowe reports that one young wife often hid bruises on her body put there by her husband. One time he grabbed her as she walked to a crafts store in Denver, lopped off her pony tail, then grabbed her throat, adding fresh bruises to her neck.

Last year he slammed her against the living room wall of their home and kicked her repeatedly in the head. He then stuffed her unconscious body into the fireplace, but she lived.

Diane Hawkins was not so fortunate. In May 1993, Diane and her daughter, Katrina Harris, were found stabbed and mutilated in their home in Washington. Hawkins, a mother of six, was disemboweled and her heart was cut out. Harris was partly decapitated. Police arrested Norman Roderick Harrell, Hawkins' ex-boyfriend, and charged him with the murders.

What is going on? Is our world to be filled with violence from here on? Jesus said in Matthew 24:37-38,

> But as the days of Noah were, so shall also the coming of the Son of Man be. For as in the days that were before the

> flood they were eating and drinking, marrying and giving in marriage, until the day that Noah entered into the ark.

This sounds like the present generation. Restaurants are on every corner, marriage as well as divorce is on the rise, and there is increasing partying and drinking as people try to drown their troubles or get a new high. However, one other clue is found in the scriptures in relation to Noah's day:

> The earth also was corrupt before God, and the earth was filled with *violence*. And God said unto Noah, The end of all flesh is come before me: for the earth is filled with *violence through them;* and, behold, I will destroy them with the earth (Genesis 6:11,13).

The "last days" Jesus spoke about in Matthew 24 are here, and prophecy is being fulfilled. It is a fact there will be violence in the land, but people can purpose to be like Noah and stay close to God in spite of the evil spirits and darkness that surround them. God spoke to Noah in Genesis 7:1, "Come thou and all thy house into the ark; for thee have I seen righteous before me in this generation."

Noah did not succumb to the pressure of his day or the influence of evil. It is possible—not only possible, but realistically so—to be able to live according to the code of ethics given in the Bible. The scripture says to be kind, respectful, and to give honor to whom honor is due. The Lord did not put conditions or terms with the commandments; they were simply to be obeyed in spite of the environment.

You may feel like your feeble effort will not make that much difference, but your effort joined with that of others can make all the difference in the world.

Frank Walcott Hutt wrote about the time there were 22 planes from a naval air station who were participating in maneuvers when the fog swept in unexpectedly. Eight of them raced immediately to landing fields, but the others were caught in a swiftly forming impenetrable blanket. Four planes crashed, one of them bursting into flames, as twelve pilots dived blindly through the fog. Two hours later only two planes were aloft. Suddenly there went out over the radio this message, "All automobile owners go to the field outside the city. Two fliers are lost in the fog and you are going to help them to land."

Soon the roads approaching the field were crowded with cars creeping through the inky blackness, hardly able to see with their feeble lights. As the cars arrived, the authorities lined them up with the cars facing inward around the field. More than 2,500 cars completely surrounded the landing strip with their lights on. The lights of no single car made much impression upon that night and fog, but the lights of 2,500 of them lighted the field so brightly that a transport pilot could go aloft and guide the two aviators down to safety.

As the radio called all cars to help in the field, this book is calling all persons to help bring back old-fashioned honor, kindness and respect. Together we can make a difference in a world that is fogged with violence, disrespect and horror. This is the day to go forward in God and function according to His code of ethics and not the ethics of the world system! The magical gift of kindness can still affect a generation that has experienced violence and hate.

David Starr Jordan wrote,

> Today is your day and mine, the only day we have, the day in which we play our part. What our part may signify in the great whole we may not understand; but we are here to play it, and now is our time. This we know: it is a part of action, not of whining. It is a part of love, not cynicism. It is for us to express love in terms of human helpfulness. [5]

It is time for each individual to help bring back kindness, honor and respect!

Ten:

Kindness vs. Evil

There is a fairy tale about a girl named Pandora. She could have anything she wanted, but there was a box in her home that she was told not to open. She would pass by it day after day wondering why she could not open it, until finally one day her curiosity overcame the command. When she went over to the box and opened it, out flew evil-faced winged creatures which represented greed, malice, hate, jealousy and suchlike. She finally managed to shut the lid, but everything escaped forever into the air except one lone evil creature that she managed to close the lid on.

It is just a fairy tale, but in reality it tells the story of the Garden of Eden. God told Adam and Eve that they could eat of any tree in the beautiful lush garden except one. Day by day they walked by the tree until finally the day came when they partook of the fruit. From that one bite sin entered the human race, unleashing malice, hate, jealousy, greed and suchlike.

In reality there is still a box that the Lord says not to open, for if one does, all sorts of spirits will fly out and attack the mind. That box is anything that does not include God's love. In that box is envy, pride, a critical spirit, fault-finding, passion to be right regardless of other people's feelings, an argumentative attitude, finger-pointing, negativism, contention and meddling.

The only way to not open the box is to be filled with God's Spirit. His Spirit gives one the power to overcome the evil spirits that inhabit the earth. Good and evil are present everywhere. The Apostle Paul spoke about the war between the two. He wrote,

> I see another law in my members, warring against the law of my mind, and bringing me into captivity to the law of sin, which is in my members. O wretched man that I am! who shall deliver me from the body of this death? I thank God through Jesus Christ our Lord. So then with the mind I myself serve the law of God; but with the flesh the law of sin (Romans 7:23-25).

So the important thing to do is walk after the things of the Spirit and not give heed to the things of the carnal man. "There is therefore now no condemnation to them which are in Christ Jesus, who walk not after the flesh, but after the Spirit" (Romans 8:1). The secret is in Christ Jesus. He promised to send a Comforter, which was the Holy Spirit, that would teach people how to live overcoming lives.

The Word of God will teach and give power to those who desire to close the lid on evil spirits. God's plan is to open your mind up to power. The devil does just the opposite. He helps fill your mind with negative thinking. Only God gives a person positive mind-power. "For God hath not given us the spirit of fear; but of power, and of love, and of a sound mind" (II Timothy 1:7).

Where love is, fear is cast out! Where love is, there is power! In order for this generation to start overcoming the evil powers that abound, there must be a renewing of minds. "Be not conformed to this world; but be ye transformed by the renewing of your mind" (Romans 12:2). The world's system must not control the actions of Christians. Our minds must be renewed by God's Spirit and Word.

The Apostle Paul instructed the Christian to be strong in the Lord and in the power of His might by putting on the whole armor of God. Why? To be able to stand against the wiles of the devil. “For we wrestle not against flesh and blood, but against principalities, against powers, against the rulers of the darkness of this world, against spiritual wickedness in high places” (Ephesians 6:12).

There are spirits that float around in the air looking for a body to inhabit. Jesus talked about them. He said,

> When the unclean spirit is gone out of a man, he walketh through dry places, seeking rest, and findeth none. Then he saith, I will return into my house from whence I came out; and when he is come, he findeth it empty, swept, and garnished. Then goeth he, and taketh with himself seven other spirits more wicked than himself, and they enter in and dwell there: and the last state of that man is worse than the first. Even so shall it be also unto this wicked generation (Matthew 12:43-45).

When Jesus cast the demon spirits out of the man from Gadarene, the spirits asked Him if they could go into the bodies of a herd of swine. “So the devils besought him, saying, If thou cast us out, suffer us to go away into the herd of swine. And he said unto them, Go. And when they were come out, they went into the herd of swine” (Matthew 8:31-32).

There are three main types of spirits: man's spirit, the devil's spirits, and God's. It is important for man to humble his spirit, repent and be cleansed by the blood of Jesus Christ, but it is just as important to be filled with God's Spirit. People open themselves up to spirits that have influence upon their mind. The Apostle Paul talked about the mind being dominated by strongholds, or things that have taken over the thought processes.

> For though we walk in the flesh, we do not war after the flesh: For the weapons of our warfare are not carnal, but mighty through God to the pulling down of strong holds; Casting down imaginations, and every high thing that exalteth itself against the knowledge of God, and bringing into captivity every thought to the obedience of Christ (II Corinthians 10:3-5).

If honor, kindness and respect are to be brought back on a national, even worldwide, scale, it will only happen when each individual submits his will, spirit and mind to Jesus Christ. In Him is power to change! One grain of sand is not much, but many grains of sand together make a beach. Likewise, it takes a joint effort to change the tide of evil that is threatening to drown us in its violence.

The good news is this: where God is, things always get better. Many believe that things are too far gone, that it is impossible to do anything now. What would it take to rekindle the fire of hope today that burned within the early church? Somehow the first church brought reformation in spite of the evil present. It could happen again. The challenge is before the church. Who will take the message of the gospel of Jesus Christ and bring light into the hell-holes in every city? Who will take it to the sophisticated derelicts and hopeless moms and dads? Will you join others around the world who are taking up the battle cry, "We will reach the world and give them the gospel! We will push back the tide of evil! Together we will make a difference!"

In order for this to happen, the church must first come together in love, showing honor and respect for one another. Suspicion, gossip and selfish ambition must be put under the blood of Jesus Christ as the love of His Spirit kindles a flame which will enable the church to show forth light to a darkened world.

Frederic W. Farrar wrote in 1895,

> A kind word of praise, of sympathy, of encouragement; it would not cost you much, yet how often does pride, or envy, or indifference prevent you from speaking it? The

cup of cold water, the barley loaves, the two farthings, how often are we too wretched and too self-absorbed to give even these! And are we not to give them because we cannot endow hospitals, or build cathedrals, or write epics? If we be in the least sincere, in the least earnest, let us be encouraged. The little gifts of our poverty, the small services of our insignificance, the barley loaves of the Galilean boy on the desert plain...are despised by the world. But they are also dear. They are accepted. They will be infinitely rewarded by Him who gives the conies their homes in the rocks; who knows every sparrow's fall; who numbers the very hairs of our heads; who builds the vast continents by the toil of the coral insect; and by His grains of sand stays the raging of the sea. [1]

Epilogue

Key of Richness

A key held within the hand may sometimes appear rusty and old.
But shining through the rust, can also be seen a glint of gold.
After rubbing and cleaning there comes a shine,
Making the key glow with a richness, extra-ordinary fine.

All mankind holds within their hand the key to abundant life,
Sometimes made dull and rusty by life's care and strife.
The gold and riches are there hidden underneath it all,
But made clear when the decision is made to answer God's call.

A call to love, service, honor, and respect for each fellow man,

A higher way of living by showing kindness to all that one can.
It is choosing whether to walk as a pauper or as a king,
Existing in a state of sadness or causing the heart to sing!

So choose well today, the path which you decide to take,
For either choice shall be rewarded by the decision you make.
The road of life is long, why live it with hate, disrespect, and sadness?
When gladness, friends, and true success fill the way of kindness!

(J. Haney)

There are ten good things for which no man has ever been sorry:

For doing good to all;
For speaking evil of no one:
For hearing before judging;
For thinking before speaking;
For holding an angry tongue;
For being kind to the distressed;
For asking pardon for all wrongs;

For being patient toward everybody;
For stopping the ear to the tale-bearer;
For dis-believing the most of evil reports. [1]

The concepts contained in this book are as old as time. With the passing of time, some of them have become tarnished. You can choose to toss them aside and join others that have done the same, but in so doing you write your own death sentence. If you pick up these principles and use them in your daily life, you will be the richest person in town, because they have blessing attached to them.

They are not ideas of grandeur glibly talked about, but they are bedrock truth that will blow away any prejudice, hate and evil. This is the day to apply the principles of Christ and become the person that God intended for you to become when you were created.

When you receive His Spirit, then you are able to do these things. "The kingdom of God is within you" (Luke 17:21). God's way is the higher road. It leads upward into excellence, blessings and power. Enlarge your world by enlarging your capacity to love, for love never fails!

Notes

Chapter 1

[1] *Reader's Digest,* July 1994, 53-56.

[2] Dale Royal, Tommy Hill, Red Sovine and J. William Denny, *Teddy Bear,* Cedarwood Publishing, 1976.

[3] Walter B. Knight, *Knight's Treasure of Illustrations* (Grand Rapids, MI: Wm. B. Eerdmans Publishing Co., 1963) 197.

[4] Ibid., 198.

[5] Ibid., 199.

[6] Ibid., 174.

[7] Dean C. Dutton, arranged and compiled, *Quests and Conquests* (Guthrie, OK: Live Service Publishing Co., 1923) #1235-F.

Chapter 2

[1] Jack Canfield and Mark Victor Hansen, *A 2nd Helping of Chicken Soup for the Soul* (Deerfield Beach, FL: Health Communications, Inc., 1993) 36.

[2] Knight, 196.

[3] Ibid., 197.

Chapter 3

[1] Knight, 216.

[2] Dutton, #1328.

[3] Paul Lee Tan, ThD., *Encyclopedia of 7,700 Illustrations: Signs of the Times* (Rockville, MD: Assurance Publishers, 1979) 1479.

[4] Ibid., 706.

[5] Dutton, #27.

[6] Ibid., #1068.

[7] Steven R. Mosley, *A Tale of Three Virtues, Cures for Colorless Christianity* (Sisters, OR: Questar Publishers, Inc., 1989) 251.

[8] Max Lucado, *No Wonder They Call Him The Saviour* (Portland, OR: Multnomah Press, 1986) 73.

[9] Joseph S. Johnson, compiled by, *A Field of Diamonds* (Nashville, TN: Broadman Press, 1974) 128.

Chapter 4

[1] Mrs. Charles E. Cowman, *Streams in the Desert, Vol. Two* (Grand Rapids, MI: Zondervan Publishing House, 1966) March 30.
[2] Tan, 131-132.
[3] Mary Sherman Hilbert, *Chicken Soup for the Soul, #3* (Deerfield Beach, Florida: Health Communications, Inc., 1996) 8.

Chapter 5

[1] Knight, 198.
[2] Clinton T. Howell, ed., *Lines to Live By* (Nashville, TN: Thomas Nelson Publishers, 1972) 35.
[3] *Reader's Digest,* March 1994, 9
[4] Ibid., 22
[5] *Time* Magazine, November 1993, 31
[6] *U.S. News & World Report,* February 14, 1994, 17.

7 *Reader's Digest,* March 1994, 49
8 Ibid., 46
9 Cowman, February 22.
10 Tan, 1475.
11 Cowman, February 16.

Chapter 6

1 Mosley, 120.
2 Dutton, #605.
3 Tan, 709.
4 Ibid., 479-480.

Chapter 7

1 *Reader's Digest,* May 1994, 73.
2 Dutton, #206.
3 Tan, 1475.
4 Johnson, 18.
5 Ibid., 16.
6 Howell, 14.
7 Johnson, 17.

[8] Cowman, June 22.

[9] Howell, 130.

[10] Ibid., 129.

Chapter 8

[1] Knight, 196.

[2] Ibid.

[3] Cowman, July 16.

Chapter 9

[1] Tan, 153.

[2] Ibid., 1653.

[3] Ibid., 621.

[4] Ibid., 153.

[5] Howell, 29.

Chapter 10

[1] Cowman, May 2.

Epilogue

[1] Howell, 29.